PRAISE FOR YOU CAN CULTURE

"Outstanding leaders prioritize cultural health for enduring success. *You Can Culture* provides an actionable guide to overcoming organizational dysfunction and sustaining a thriving culture through timeless leadership habits. A must-read for every leader!"
FRANK BLAKE, former CEO, The Home Depot; board member, Macy's Inc.

"*You Can Culture* is not just a compelling read, it's also a transformative journey that empowers you to evolve into the leader you aspire to be. By taking small, yet significant steps to integrate the habits and practices outlined in this book, you'll build a thriving culture that drives results and positively impacts both people and the planet."
DR. MARSHALL GOLDSMITH, *Thinkers50* #1 executive coach and *New York Times* bestselling author of *The Earned Life, Triggers,* and *What Got You Here Won't Get You There*

"Tobias has confronted the worst and the best of organizational culture and has drawn vital lessons for the future. Executives, while laser-focused on creating value, often overlook the importance of sharing values, with devastating consequences. *You Can Culture* is a leader's guide to prioritizing and cultivating clarity and integrity around what matters most. In a world facing headwinds of enormous magnitude, this is a necessary book."
BERTRAND BADRÉ, former group CFO and managing director, The World Bank

"*You Can Culture* is a helpful guide for every leader striving to drive change and cultivate a values-based corporate culture, and a reminder that while cultural health doesn't come for free, it is well worth the investment."
MARIA HEMBERG, former chief legal officer and general counsel, Volvo Cars

"*You Can Culture* isn't your typical coffee-table book displayed in corporate offices, it's a guide designed for action—belonging in the 'workout place.' Tobias Sturesson presents an honest proposition: it is possible to make a genuine impact on organizational culture and leadership, but it requires hard work and persistence—it's not a temporary project. If you're ready to roll up your sleeves and commit to transforming your workplace culture, this book will be an impactful guide."
KLAUS MOOSMAYER, chief ethics, risk, and compliance officer and member of the executive committee, Novartis

"Tobias Sturesson has dedicated his career to helping leaders build thriving cultures, and it shows. *You Can Culture* is something unusual—raw and deeply personal, as Tobias candidly shares his experiences within toxic environments, with numerous practical examples from organizations of all sizes that are immensely actionable and thoroughly researched. Start your transformative journey through *You Can Culture*. You won't regret it!"

JOSH LINKNER, five-time tech entrepreneur, *New York Times* bestselling author, and venture capitalist

"Sturesson pulls multiple strands together in this well-laid-out guide to culture renewal: his extensive work with leadership teams and companies, the insights he's gained from conversations with renowned researchers and practitioners, and the lessons he's learned as someone who has personally experienced the pull that deeply harmful cultures can have on us. It's a valuable resource for leaders who desire to build trusted and thriving organizations."

SANDRA SUCHER, professor of management practice, Harvard Business School; author of *The Power of Trust*

"Everybody talks about culture, but there's very little good, practical literature on exactly how to do it. If you're a leader, you MUST culture, and this book is a great guide for your journey."

ROB CHESNUT, former chief ethics officer and general counsel, Airbnb; author of *Intentional Integrity*

"In *You Can Culture*, Tobias Sturesson gives us a deeply compelling book. It grabs a reader from the first sentence with a fearless personal revelation, then moves into many pages of well-considered, actionable tactics for improving the performance of your employee culture. And yet, this remarkable book never loses sight of the humanity that cultures represent and the ultimate responsibility of the enterprise to protect it. This book is worth reading, recommending, and reading again."

STAN SLAP, *New York Times* bestselling author of *Under the Hood: Fire Up and Fine-Tune Your Employee Culture* and *Bury My Heart at Conference Room B*

"Culture profoundly influences every aspect of an organization—whether people collaborate effectively, take ownership of the mission, voice critical concerns, or innovate with their best ideas. In *You Can Culture*, Tobias Sturesson offers a compelling blend of research-backed strategies, profound personal stories, and actionable advice, empowering leaders to uphold essential values and cultivate thriving cultures that drive sustainable results."

MEGAN REITZ, adjunct professor of leadership and dialogue, Hult Business School; author of *Speak Up*; *Thinkers50* ranked thinker 2023

"In today's rapidly changing business landscape, many organizations recognize the vital importance of evolving their culture to align with strategic goals and core values. Yet, many leaders often find it easier to delegate the change challenge to HR to 'fix,' instead of taking charge. In *You Can Culture*, Tobias Sturesson offers a practical guide to change, with actionable steps that every leader can take to foster a thriving culture. By cultivating these timeless leadership habits, you'll see tangible results . . . and your team and organization will thank you for it!"

SIOBHAN MCHALE, executive general manager: people, culture, and change at DuluxGroup; author of *The Insider's Guide to Culture Change*

"Tobias's passion for fostering healthy organizations is truly inspiring. His profound knowledge is evident as he draws upon personal lessons learned the hard way, and insights from academic and professional communities. Building responsible organizations is hard work, and *You Can Culture* doesn't offer shortcuts or quick fixes. Instead, this excellent book serves as a practical guide to achieving lasting impact and genuine change. It's an essential read for any professional interested in building responsible organizations."

ANNA ROMBERG, executive vice president of sustainability, legal, and compliance, Getinge; cofounder of The Nordic Business Ethics Initiative

"Hands down, no corporate BS, a very useful book! This book has been seven years in the making, but Tobias has not been idle. He has used this time to learn from all the best thought leaders, scientists, researchers, and authors in leadership, human behavior, and culture, and he is packing it all into this book so that we don't have to. A book that is intelligent, practical, and easy to translate into action!"

MICHAELA AHLBERG, chief ethics and compliance officer, Getinge

"Starting with a personal story that will knock your socks off, Tobias Sturesson integrates his own experience and wisdom with examples from successful organizations and experts to provide an engaging, easy-to-digest, and practical guide to building and maintaining a healthy organizational culture. What I most appreciated was Sturesson's wisdom that healthy cultures can't be created with short-term, optics-focused initiatives or quick fixes. Instead, Sturesson provides a roadmap for creating healthy cultures by doing the hard work every day, repeatedly taking steps that turn the espoused into the lived."

JIM DETERT, professor of business administration at the University of Virginia's Darden School of Business and author of *Choosing Courage: The Everyday Guide to Being Brave at Work*

"When done right, culture is the most powerful competitive advantage we need to thrive, win, and build unstoppable momentum. In *You Can Culture*, Tobias provides a vital playbook for heart-based leaders, culture champions, and every one of us who strives to make purposeful decisions and values-led actions. Get this book, it's the best decision you can make!"

PAUL EPSTEIN, former NFL and NBA executive and bestselling author of *Better Decisions Faster* and *The Power of Playing Offense*

"*You Can Culture* is an accessible, yet profound read, filled with compelling stories and eye-opening insights to help any leader lead better."

BOB LANGERT, retired VP of sustainability, McDonald's Corporation; author of *The Battle to Do Good*

"In *You Can Culture*, Tobias Sturesson offers readers a journey through the real-life experiences of numerous organizational leaders dealing with reputational risk, scandal, and toxic cultures—and via his own personal and compelling story of challenge and redemption—in order to distill a short list of mindsets and everyday practices that can place leaders on a path to building and sustaining healthy, ethical, and effective organizations. This readable book is both practical and inspiring!"

MARY C. GENTILE, professor of ethics, UVA Darden School of Business; author of *Giving Voice to Values*

"Given the frequent corporate scandals in the news, there is an urgent need for integrity in leadership for any company that seeks to be trusted. Yet, while managing ethics and fostering cultural health are vital, many leaders lack the necessary skills. *You Can Culture* is a clarion call to care for your culture and offers an immensely practical toolbox to get it done. If you want to keep your company from ending up in the news for the wrong reasons, pick up this book today!"

GUIDO PALAZZO, professor of business ethics at the University of Lausanne

"Cultural health is vital for strategy execution, value alignment, and attracting top talent. Yet many managers lack the tools to shape it effectively. *You Can Culture* offers a practical guide to developing leadership habits that will transform your team and company culture."

MELISSA DAIMLER, chief learning officer at Udemy and author of *ReCulturing: Design Your Company Culture to Connect with Strategy and Purpose for Lasing Success*

"This book identifies the leadership qualities required of anyone serious about changing an organization's culture. A must-read for culture change practitioners."

JAY BARNEY, strategic management professor, David Eccles School of Business; coauthor of *The Secret of Culture Change*

"While companies and organizations can indeed be a powerful force for good, achieving true transformation requires leaders to prioritize long-term, concrete actions over mere talk or temporary solutions. In *You Can Culture*, Tobias Sturesson draws on his harrowing experience in a toxic environment and extensive expertise in helping leaders cultivate thriving cultures to present four evidence-based leadership habits that will not only enhance your organization's success, but also empower it to become a force for good in the world and promote workplace flourishing. Embrace this invaluable gift!"

EMMA IHRE, head of sustainability, Embracer Group

"The world is teeming with kitschy handbooks and crude recipes for changing organizational culture, as though it were simple and straightforward. We've known for decades that leaders who ignore toxic cultures do so at their own peril. But, if you happen to be a leader who understands that shaping and sustaining a healthy culture is critical for your strategy and long-term success, you're holding one of the best guidebooks (by one of the best guides) you could have. Keep this book close at hand, study it, wrestle with it, and before long, you will see a vibrancy in your organization you never imagined possible."

RON CARUCCI, managing partner, Navalent; author of *To Be Honest*

"Tobias's voice is cogent, informed, passionate, and authentic. This compelling and powerful book can truly make a difference for new and experienced leaders alike."

STEVEN ROGELBERG, PhD, chancellor's professor, UNC Charlotte; author of *Glad We Met: The Art and Science of One-on-One Meetings*

"*You Can Culture* is both enlightening and accessible. The dissection of corporate culture is based on academic research, which Tobias imparts to the reader in an understandable and informed manner. His extensive experience with corporate culture provides the reader with practical tools for implementation vital to building flourishing and ethical organizations."

ANN TENBRUNSEL, professor of business ethics, department chair, management and organization, Mendoza College of Business; coauthor of *Blind Spots: Why We Fail to Do What's Right and What to Do about It*

"This book offers a powerful blend of actionable, practical advice for leaders seeking to shape culture, alongside compelling stories and insights from experienced leaders and culture experts. Tobias tells a captivating story—I was gripped from page one by his personal culture journey. I highly recommend this book to anyone who knows that culture matters and seeks actionable strategies to contribute to a better and healthier culture in their organization."

CAROLYN TAYLOR, culture change pioneer and author of *Walking the Talk: Building a Culture for Success*

an imprint of Amplify Publishing Group

www.amplifypublishinggroup.com

You Can Culture: Transformative Leadership Habits
for a Thriving Workplace, Positive Impact, and Lasting Success

For more information, please contact:
Amplify Publishing, an imprint of Amplify Publishing Group
620 Herndon Parkway, Suite 220
Herndon, VA 20170
info@amplifypublishing.com

Library of Congress Control Number: 2024907314

CPSIA Code: PRV0624A

ISBN-13: 979-8-89138-154-4

Printed in the United States

To my wife, Lena: without your courage, wisdom, and support, this book would surely never have been written.

To my mom: you endured so much, yet rose up to fight for others.

And to the many leaders who daily sacrifice to uphold your values, serve your team members, and steward the mission of your organization.

With gratitude.

YOU CAN CULTURE

Transformative Leadership Habits for a Thriving Workplace, Positive Impact, and Lasting Success

TOBIAS STURESSON

amplify
an imprint of Amplify Publishing Group

Contents

Habit 3
Get Listening   **159**

Habit 4
Get Integrity   **209**

Introduction

My Journey from Toxic Cult to Cultural Transformation

There may be times when we are powerless to prevent injustice,
but there must never be a time when we fail to protest.[1]

—Elie Wiesel, professor, Holocaust survivor, and Nobel laureate

O n a late summer night in 2008, I was confronted with a terrible truth I had desperately tried to escape. I was watching a prime-time investigative program on Swedish television. While the image on the TV screen was blurred and the individual's voice was distorted to protect her anonymity, I watched my own mother tell a national broadcast audience how she, as a member of a Christian community that gradually turned into a religious cult, became isolated and demonized, and even tried to take her own life as a way to escape from the terror and the trauma.

I grew up in that community, learned to revere its manipulative founder, and became part of its destructive culture, even as it tore our family apart.

Complicit in Psychological Abuse

I was raised in a family passionate about helping people in need. My mom was a social worker, and my dad was building a fledgling IT business. At the age of eleven, our lives took a significant turn when my parents gave up city life to help establish a Christian church and community center in a small village. Guided by the inspiring vision of a charismatic founder to serve people's needs holistically, the community grew and became the focal point of our family's life. My mother joined the leadership team, and I was groomed to become somewhat of the founder's right hand. We worked hard and were excited to serve the many visitors who came, often from impoverished situations, seeking joy, fellowship, and adventure at the center.

Regrettably, the founder became increasingly manipulative and erratic, and the culture turned toxic, marred by fear and silence. As many departed, those of us who stayed grew more devoted and increasingly isolated from the broader religious community.

And then the nightmare began. The founder targeted individuals he perceived as threats (which could include anyone for whatever reason, even his own family), subjecting them to isolation, demonization, and public shame.

I avoided the horror of being targeted by partaking in the psychological abuse of others.

In 2002 the founder set his sights on my mother. In a twisted plot reminiscent of a movie thriller, he enlisted me to become a part of the psychological abuse, simultaneously assigning me the task of keeping her from hurting herself when the pain and trauma became too much to bear. I complied. After numerous failed suicide attempts, my mom became a high-risk patient in a psychiatric ward. There, she finally found the strength to follow in my dad's footsteps and break free from the community. However, it took several more years before I summoned the courage to make my own escape.

The Cover-Up

The investigative TV program and a book telling my mother's story triggered countless newspaper articles and a public outcry. The community's board of directors, of which I was then a part, sprang into action to save our reputation and protect the founder. We penned a press statement with a vague apology to people hurt by our "sometimes insensitive treatment" done with the "intention of helping people." Sadly, it served as a cover-up, allowing us to rationalize our decision to stay. We claimed to have dealt with the past, even though we hadn't nearly acknowledged the harm caused or confronted the toxic culture and leadership.

However, I was left with a growing internal dissonance. As I became increasingly vocal in questioning the culture and our approach to the past, I finally made the frightening decision I should have made many years earlier—I walked out the door, never to return.

Consequences of Cultural Challenges

How could an organization seemingly driven by a noble mission become so toxic? And how did I, someone who perceived myself as an ethical and values-driven leader, become complicit in psychological abuse?

These questions have haunted and compelled me since I left that destructive community, and I later dedicated my professional life to advocating for cultural health.

In 2017, after spending many years as the CEO of a communications agency, my wife and I cofounded Heart Management, a culture change and leadership development agency, with the vision of contributing to a world where organizations with a healthy culture are the norm rather than the exception.

Over the last several years, our team has been in the trenches supporting executives and managers in numerous start-ups, small and medium-sized enterprises, multinational corporations, governmental organizations, and international nongovernmental organizations (NGOs). They wanted to build a thriving workplace and a culture that delivers and needed to successfully overcome critical issues such as a crisis of trust after a scandal, lack of cohesiveness after a merger or acquisition, lack of quality culture, patterns of unhelpful or destructive behavior, lack of alignment around values, or a culture of silence.

While I'm obviously glad that few organizations end up as religious cults, there is an epidemic of unhealthy workplace culture today. It has become so prevalent that it's the topic of a growing number of TV series. While it can make for great TV, the real-world consequences are severe, destroying tremendous company value and even wrecking people's lives.

A lack of cultural health weakens resilience and gives rise to disengagement, division, dysfunction, silence, and destructive behavioral patterns—hindering you from delivering on your mission and strategy and eroding trust with your team, clients, and other crucial stakeholders. Let's look at a few disturbing statistics:

- In 2022 an extensive study published by the Massachusetts Institute of Technology (MIT) identified toxic culture to be the main driver behind the Great Resignation in 2021.[2]

- Disengagement cost companies $8.8 trillion in lost productivity in 2023.[3]
- A 2019 study revealed that one in five Americans left a job in the last five years because of bad culture, costing companies an estimated $223 billion.[4]
- Cultural challenges are a key reason mergers and acquisitions fail.[5]
- While 91 percent of business executives agree that building and maintaining trust improves the bottom line, only 27 percent of customers and 65 percent of employees agree they highly trust their company. About half of consumers and employees report experiencing a trust-damaging event. A majority of them reported that they ended their relationship with the company after the experience.[6]

Why I Felt Compelled to Write This Book

Cardiovascular disease is the leading cause of death globally, and studies show that we often fail to pay adequate attention to our physical heart health. Sadly, I've found the same to be true about the health of our organizational culture.

As the host of the *Leading Transformational Change* podcast, I've interviewed numerous renowned economists, ethics researchers, management professors, and behavioral scientists; learned from senior executives at famous corporations; and spoken to insiders involved with some of the world's most infamous corporate scandals to understand how reputable and seemingly highly successful companies could end up in crisis and scandal. And how, like an impending heart failure, the leadership seldom saw it coming.

I discovered that while senior leaders are often rightly laser-focused on maximizing financial performance, being attractive to external stakeholders, and mitigating reputational risks, they often fail to give enough attention to the vital health of their culture even though, like our heart, it can help us thrive even in challenges or hinder us from achieving our most important objectives.

Considering the widespread prevalence and destructive consequences of cultural challenges, why do leaders often fail to deal with them before they have significant consequences? To answer that, we're going to take a quick look at three destructive yet common myths that leaders love to believe, even though they keep us blind and paralyzed.

Myth No. 1: The Health Illusion

Just as we often assume that our physical heart is healthy, we take for granted that we are a good organization with a healthy culture and great values, making us oblivious to the need to check our cultural health and leading us to use our values as a shield to protect against criticism. However, as we'll explore in chapter 2, we are often not as values-driven as we want to assume.

Myth No. 2: The Bad Apple Fallacy

When faced with symptoms of a lack of cultural health, there is a tendency to attribute the problem to one or a few difficult or destructive employees or a corrupt leader, leading to an oversight of broader cultural challenges and reluctance to take ownership. However, culture is always cocreated. There was someone who knew but didn't speak up or someone who was told but didn't act.

Myth No. 3: Culture as a Project

When we see the need to address a lack of cultural health, often prompted by internal or external pressure, there is a tendency to relegate the issue to human resources (HR) or ethics and compliance, expecting them to initiate a short-term project—a new set of values, a training program, an employer branding initiative, or an event with an inspiring speaker. However, studies show that only 15 percent of these culture transformation initiatives succeed,[7] often making a dark situation look even bleaker as fickle hope fades out.

But what if I could show you a much more effective way to overcome cultural challenges and transform your cultural health?

A Radically More Effective Approach to Culture Change

While researching this book, I googled "the world's healthiest person." I was surprised that the top result featured a remarkably fit ninety-six-year-old man in a running shirt. The late Mr. Charles Eugster was known as the world's fittest pensioner before he passed away in 2017.[8] At eighty-seven, he took up bodybuilding; at ninety-three, he took up sprinting and broke several world records. So what was his secret? Eugster told *Vice* magazine, "You see, the stupid thing is that people don't realize that you can have a beach body at ninety . . . I am living proof that, if you eat right and exercise properly, you can be that guy at any age."[9] He also bragged about how seventy-year-old ladies on the beach would turn their heads when he passed by.

Eugster understood what is evident to us all—that sustainable habits, not short-term initiatives or Instagram posts from the gym, are the keys to physical health and a resilient heart.

The same holds true for our cultural health.

Cultural health—which enables us to deliver on our mission and strategy, create a thriving workplace, and have a responsible impact—is not primarily built by short-term culture initiatives or events but by the everyday leadership habits that signal what is valued, rewarded, or disregarded in our team or organization.

To change our culture, we must make small but critical changes to what we repeatedly do instead of putting all our hope in occasional efforts.

When we, as leaders, are willing to begin by changing our habits and behaviors instead of deflecting blame, we can make a significant difference.

The Four Culture-Building Habits of Values-Driven Leaders

Through our work with hundreds of leaders in numerous organizations and extensive research over many years, we've discovered that, just like the heart has four chambers, there are four vital culture-building habits that will transform your cultural health. They aren't complex, but they are challenging. They will push your comfort zone, and you can't relegate them to someone else. As a leader, you have to take ownership and be the change. While the practical application and tactical incorporation may need to vary based on cultural and historical contexts, I am convinced that the habits are timeless and universally relevant to leaders across all contexts.

Habit 1: Get Humble

As leaders, we will, at times, realize that we have acted in conflict with our mission or values, become a part of hindering behavioral patterns, or begun to accept a lack of cultural health. When these issues are hidden, disregarded, or not dealt with consistently and urgently, there is a risk of breaking trust and impairing our ability to fulfill the mission, build a thriving workplace, and have a responsible impact. However, by embracing vulnerability, taking ownership, and actively working to repair broken trust, we can avoid pitfalls and transform our cultural health.

Habit 2: Get Clear

Many values statements are vague, disconnected from the mission, and seldom prioritized or consistently adhered to, leading to a lack of integrity and clarity around cultural priorities and hindering strategy execution. To build and sustain cultural health, we must clarify our most important values, celebrate the right behaviors, and deal with unhelpful or destructive behavior.

Habit 3: Get Listening

When team members don't speak up or their voices go unheard, we lose critical insight into dilemmas, concerns, and opportunities for learning, improvement, and growth. As leaders, we often overestimate our listening ability and underestimate how hard it can be to give feedback or raise concerns. To break the silence, transform our cultural health, and avoid pitfalls, we must get listening by soliciting feedback, creating conditions for brave conversations, and exercising voicing our values.

Habit 4: Get Integrity

Too often there's conflict between the values we claim and the signals we send. We might, for example, say we want teamwork but incentivize only individual performance. To avoid mixed signals, we must ensure that the stories we tell, the rituals we design, and the processes and incentives we set embody our mission and values and sustain our cultural health.

Grow Your Leadership to Transform Your Culture

Having worked with hundreds of leaders through our culture and leadership programs, I've realized that many of their questions echoed my own:

- How did our culture develop these unhelpful or destructive behavioral patterns?
- What drove me to act in conflict with the values I claim or remain silent when witnessing unacceptable behavior?

And the more practical but equally critical questions:

- How can I bring about needed cultural and behavioral change in my team?
- How can I be a more values-driven leader, leave a positive legacy, and avoid becoming blinded when the pressure is on?
- How can I help build a thriving workplace with highly engaged team members who deliver on our mission and strategy?

I dedicated seven years to writing this book to offer an honest, extensively researched, and actionable guide for people who aspire to be great leaders who build remarkable cultures. It serves as a comprehensive culture and leadership program for the price of one book. The culture-building habits and practices I present are relevant and critical whether you lead a small team or a large organization.

This book provides you with:
- a twelve-month journey to become a more intentionally values-driven leader and cultivate a thriving workplace and a culture that delivers,
- twelve monthly practices to deliberately develop the four culture-building habits, and

- thought-provoking questions for personal or group reflection and concrete actions to facilitate change and growth.

In this book, you will learn from:

- my personal journey and leadership experience, failures, and triumphs;
- numerous other leaders at every level, with whom we've been fortunate to work over the years (their stories are edited slightly to protect their anonymity);
- my conversations with senior executives who have helped shape culture at well-known companies such as McDonald's, Airbnb, IKEA, the Home Depot, Volvo Cars, and Mars;
- seven years of extensive research and interviews with over fifty renowned researchers and experts in management, culture, economy, ethics, and behavioral science; and
- insiders and whistleblowers involved in high-profile corporate scandals.

I'm confident that your journey through this book will help you become a more effective, values-driven leader, better equipped to cultivate a thriving workplace and a culture that delivers.

Not the End but a New Beginning

After spending two years in a psychiatric ward, my mother mended her heart. She became an advocate for healthier cultures as a senior leader in the public sector. And I'm very grateful to say that she's been one of the most ardent supporters of our mission and the message of this book.

A decade after watching that fateful TV program on Swedish television, I was invited to help an international NGO facing a public scandal that had uncovered grave cultural issues and led to a crisis of trust and severe financial challenges. But instead of deflecting blame, the new leadership chose to do the work of practicing the four culture-building habits. Though the process was challenging, it led to a remarkable transformation, giving me unshakable hope that restoring cultural health is possible and the conviction that *you can culture*! This is your invitation to take that transformational journey.

However, to prepare you to develop the four vital habits, we will now set the foundation by exploring: culture essentials, why you might not be as values-driven as you'd like to think, and how you can best plan your journey to get the most out of this book.

Prepare for Transformation

1

Understanding Culture Essentials

The biggest danger in trying to understand
culture is to oversimplify it.[1]

—Edgar H. Schein, professor emeritus of the
MIT Sloan School of Management

I t had been a massive undertaking. They had facilitated numerous
workshops with thousands of employees based on a process
designed by a communications agency. In each workshop, participants selected from an aspirational list of values and behaviors the
agency had put together—words such as "integrity," "teamwork,"
and "innovation." The goal was to identify the top three options.
These would be implemented as the organization's new core values.
However, as the process continued, HR and senior executives began
questioning whether this would bring the change they sought or if
it was a dead end. That's when they contacted our team at Heart
Management. In our conversations, I quickly realized that they
cared deeply about their mission and that while they had many

things to be proud of, certain elements of their culture hindered them from collaborating and innovating to better serve their stakeholders and deliver on their strategy.

We decided to gather their entire executive management team for a culture vision kickoff to ensure they had a robust and shared understanding of culture and a vision for the change they wanted to achieve. I met a room of well-educated and experienced executives leading this over ten-thousand-strong organization. However, despite their good intentions, it quickly became apparent that they had embraced the culture-as-a-project myth. And that at the heart of the issue was a too simplistic understanding of culture.

During the kickoff, we discussed what culture is, how it works, and why merely defining a new set of values wouldn't bring the desired change on its own. They defined a vision for their culture and reflected on the role that senior leadership plays and why they shouldn't relegate the responsibility to HR. Afterward, they told me that the workshop was a game changer. As their understanding of culture evolved, their approach and strategy did as well. From a short-term, programmatic mindset, they realized that culture wasn't another checkbox they should try to tick off but a dynamic organism they needed to care for. And they courageously set out a new course to better their cultural health, including initiating a research project with a leading institution to innovate ways to measure the adoption of values-driven behaviors in a large and complex organization.

To strengthen our cultural health, we must first ensure that we have a good understanding of what culture is, how it works, and why it matters to our ability to deliver results, cultivate a thriving workplace, and have a responsible impact. In this chapter, we will take a look at the following:

- Exploring the heart of culture
- Ten culture insights
- The three hallmarks of cultural health

But before we jump in, let's take a brief pause and reflect.

REFLECTION

How would you define culture? I've asked hundreds of leaders that same question. Take two minutes to reflect on the question and write down your answer. I'm going to ask you to do the same thing later in this chapter.

Exploring the Heart of Culture

Today almost every business magazine and conference deals with organizational culture in some way, yet many leaders feel that culture is hard to define and understand. Harvard professor Boris Groysberg and colleagues stated, "Executives are often confounded by culture, because much of it is anchored in unspoken behaviors, mindsets, and social patterns."[2] While it may not seem like a significant problem, misconceptions and myths about culture tend to make us chase things that don't matter and overlook other things that do.

After studying, working on, and reading obsessively about culture for many years, I've come to define it as

"how our group thinks, relates, and works to achieve success based on shared beliefs and assumptions."

There's a lot to unpack in that statement, and to do that, we're going to explore a few insightful culture definitions from leading researchers and practitioners, many of whom you'll meet later in this book. As you read these definitions, I encourage you to reflect on how they might inform your own understanding of culture. Remember, you can culture!

1 **Artifacts, espoused values, and underlying assumptions**
The late Professor Emeritus Edgar Schein, known as the father of modern culture research, describes three levels of culture: (1) artifacts, (2) espoused values, and (3) underlying assumptions. The artifacts—"what you see, hear, and feel as you hang around in the organization"[3] (e.g., the way the office is organized, the way people dress, the jokes people make)—are the easiest to recognize. The espoused values are those that the organization claims and promotes (and might have printed on posters). However, to truly understand a culture, Schein believed you need to recognize the underlying assumptions—the deeply ingrained unconscious beliefs and perceptions that guide the behavior and decision-making within an organization.

2 **An organization's tacit social order**
Professor Boris Groysberg and colleagues offer this description: "Culture is the tacit social order of an organization: It shapes attitudes and behaviors in wide-ranging and durable ways. Cultural norms define what is encouraged, discouraged, accepted, or rejected within a group."[4]

3 All about patterns

Siobhan McHale, head of people, culture, and change at DuluxGroup and author of *The Insider's Guide to Culture Change*, wrote that culture is "all about patterns of thinking and relating that tell people how to behave in an organization. And these patterns start to take hold the first day that people walk into the workplace."[5]

4 A strategy execution engine

Professor Jennifer Chatman, a renowned culture researcher and codirector of the Berkeley Culture Center, told me that "culture is the strategy execution engine"[6] of the organization.

5 A living organism that gathers information

Stan Slap—bestselling author of *Under the Hood* and founder of SLAP Company, which helps companies such as Google, Microsoft, and Starbucks create committed cultures—offered his unique but insightful definition of culture: "Culture is a living organism that constantly gathers information to confirm its perception of reality, ensure its survival and emotional well-being."[7]

6 An organization's core business

One of my favorite statements on the impact of culture comes from Carolyn Taylor, a culture change pioneer and author of *Walking the Talk*: "Culture is what you do every time you make a decision. Culture is what causes your projects to run over budget, your strategies never to be implemented, your customers to get frustrated and walk away and your business to be blind to a major threat until it knocks you over. Culture is your business, not something you have on the side."[8]

Ten Culture Insights

We've now looked at what culture is. The next question then is what that means for your leadership, team, and organization and why it matters. We will explore the answers to these questions through the following ten culture insights:

1   **Culture can either enable or limit the success of your team and organization.**
    Culture is not created by mandate but is shaped through interactions. Whether or not we've defined a set of values, we still have a culture. Our culture will determine our ability to collaborate, innovate, deliver high-quality products or services, garner the trust of customers and other important stakeholders, and avoid ethical risks, among other factors.

2   **Culture is formed to cope with uncertainty.**
    Picture going to a new country or a party at your spouse's or friend's workplace. As you enter the new social situation, you will look for cues to understand the norms and behavioral patterns. How do people enter the room? How do they greet one another? Are there rituals you need to be aware of? As people join a new organization, they will, in the same way, look for cues to what would make them successful and avoid embarrassing themselves in that environment. This way of coping with uncertainty will come to define our culture.

3 Culture is cocreated.

Culture is not one person's or two people's behavior or merely the sum of each person's traits in a group. As we shape culture, we are also shaping a shared context. We take on roles and create behavioral patterns. Similar to watching a dance performance and focusing our attention on an individual dancer's movements, disregarding the larger pattern and the diverse roles being played, we may be tempted to solely focus on the behavior of one or a few team members, overlooking the behavioral pattern and the roles we have taken on within it.

4 Culture is shaped by signals.

Culture is shaped by signals of what is encouraged and rewarded, not accepted or tolerated within a team or organization. Leadership has a significant impact on these signals. However, processes, rituals, and incentives also play an essential part.

5 The values we claim might not be our enacted values.

Every culture has priorities and values and holds different assumptions and beliefs about what should be prioritized and what leads to success. However, these enacted values might significantly differ from the espoused values we advertise on our website. Therefore, we cannot take for granted that the values we promote correctly describe our culture.

6 **Don't assume you have one culture.**

Your organization might have distinct subcultures influenced by, for example, departments, locations, professions, or historical contexts. While it's naive to try to mandate that every part must have the same culture, it's still very possible to operate by shared values.

7 **Culture is both continually evolving and not easily changed.**

Assumptions and beliefs are often deeply held because they deal with what we believe has made us successful in the past. At the same time, our culture keeps evolving as our organization grows, develops, and adds or replaces leaders and team members.

8 **Culture is not solely HR or ethics and compliance's responsibility.**

While the HR and ethics and compliance functions have important roles in contributing to the health of the culture (through the processes they own and their role in supporting leaders and team members), they cannot "own" culture simply because they don't own many of the vital decisions and signals that shape the culture within the organization.

9 **Don't assume you know your culture.**

It's easy to assume that we know, understand, and would be able to accurately describe and assess our organizational or team culture. However, since our culture is our social context, we often understand it less than we think. The perspective and experience of the culture will also differ significantly depending on whether you're a frontline worker or the CEO. In a 2019 study on why culture change efforts often fail, research company Gartner identified two main reasons: (1) a lack of unfiltered data reaching leadership and (2) that companies, when describing their culture, often resort to a generic, *overused set of adjectives.*[9] To better understand our culture, we need to assess it by soliciting feedback from across the organization. (I will give some pointers on that in Practice 12.)

10 Culture is not a project.

Projects have an allure to them. They make topics such as culture seem a bit less fuzzy. We can set a clear time frame, identify a list of activities, and then measure whether we have accomplished them. It gives us the impression that we are making progress and allows us to believe we can tick culture off the list and move on to the next project. However, these should never be our goals. Culture is always evolving, and it constantly needs our attention and intentional effort.

REFLECTION

Before we move forward, I encourage you to reflect again on your understanding of culture. Remember, culture is "how our group thinks, relates, and works to achieve success based on shared beliefs and assumptions."

- How would you now define culture?
- What has shifted in your perspective?

The Three Hallmarks of Cultural Health

We've now explored what culture is and the significance it has for our leadership, our team, and our organization. If you, like me, have experienced somewhat unhealthy or perhaps even toxic cultures, you know what that might look and feel like. You've experienced the frustration, the pit in your stomach, and the fear that things might never change. However, I'm sure many of you have also experienced cultural health. You've felt the joy of collaboration unencumbered by divisive internal politics or inflated egos. You've felt the safety to speak up and share innovative ideas.

So what defines cultural health? As is true about our physical health, cultural health is not a perfect state we achieve but a continuous pursuit that is largely decided by our habits. Cultural health enables us to *deliver on our mission, cultivate a workplace where team members thrive, and have a responsible impact*. Let's explore the three hallmarks of cultural health in greater depth.

Mission Success

Ability to successfully deliver on our mission, strategy, and critical objectives

Thriving Workplace

An attractive workplace where team members can thrive and do their best work

Responsible Impact

Responsible decisions and behaviors that build stakeholder trust

Objectives

- Increase customer satisfaction and loyalty

- Increase productivity

- Foster collaboration

- Enhance continuous improvement and innovation

- Attract and retain top and diverse talent

- Build high-performing teams

- Increase employee well-being and engagement

- Increase trust with critical stakeholders

- Deliver high-quality products/services

- Make more ethical and sustainable decisions and avoid risks

Questions for assessing the health of our culture

- Do our team members take accountability for results?

- Are we focused on the mission or burdened by a lack of clarity, division, or dysfunction?

- Do we encourage learning, new ideas, and initiatives?

- Do we promote relevant collaboration?

- Do we have a healthy feedback culture?

- Do our team members feel like their contributions are valued and recognized?

- Do our team members clearly understand how to contribute to the mission and abide by our values?

- Do we have a respectful, inclusive, and psychologically safe environment?

- Is there a healthy work-life balance?

- Do our team members feel safe voicing their concerns?

- Do our leaders embody the values we claim?

- Do we deal with or gloss over unhelpful and destructive behavior (or make exceptions for high performers)?

- Are we as transparent as possible, or is there a culture of secrecy?

While this is not an exhaustive list, I'm sure you are convinced of the benefits of cultural health. I'm equally certain that improving the health of your culture in one or several of those areas could make a significant difference for your team or organization. Despite this being true for every leader I've encountered, it's astonishing how often we fail in our efforts, even when we have good intentions.

In the next chapter, we'll explore the danger of assuming that we're values-driven and why this flawed assumption might keep us from improving our cultural health.

2

The Problem with Values-Driven Leadership

If only there were evil people somewhere insidiously committing
evil deeds, and it were necessary only to separate them from
the rest of us and destroy them. But the line dividing good
and evil cuts through the heart of every human being.[1]

—Aleksandr Solzhenitsyn, writer, Soviet
dissident, and Nobel laureate

While Titus Marimi was asleep on a train on his way home from work, customs officers stopped him as he crossed the border between Denmark and Sweden. (A bridge connects the two countries.) In his recollection of the events, the customs officers forced him to undress in a windowless room and then harassed him physically, making racist comments with a sexual undertone. Marimi pressed charges against the customs officers for discriminatory behavior. This began a long legal battle.

However, several months later, in August 2020, Marimi's story reached a reporter from *Dagens Nyheter*, a major Swedish newspaper. The reporter interviewed the assistant chief of law enforcement at the customs office. Answering the question on whether Marimi's story of racist treatment could be true, she replied,

> "We train our staff to have an objective view of the people we investigate. As a government organization, we have core values that clearly state that you must be responsible and objective. We also have our own set of core values, which state that our staff has to treat people professionally. Objectivity and everyone's equal value are guidelines for our entire operation."[2]

The journalist pressed further and asked whether she believed their values and the ethics training their employees received meant they never did anything wrong. "Yes, I would say that. We never do anything wrong," she answered.

"Can a set of words make employees spotless?"[3] a journalist asked rhetorically later the same month, wanting me to comment on the infamous interview with the senior executive at the Swedish customs office. While I'm sure you, like me, would find that assertion ridiculous, leaders often assume that their noble organizational values automatically make them part of a good organization with a healthy culture, as if the values possessed some magical powers. And it's not just the Swedish customs office. My friend Michaela Ahlberg, who's built up the ethics and compliance function at several large multinational companies, told me in a 2020 interview: "Many companies assume that they have a wonderful culture, but they have never really made an assessment to see what kind of company they are."[4]

In the process of writing this book, my original Texas-based publisher collapsed in a matter of just a few weeks—a shock to both me and many of the two hundred employees. The company had grown fast, been celebrated as a best place to work, and boasted modern and conscious leadership. They made bold claims on their website about adhering to their values in all their actions. Yet it became clear in the aftermath that there hadn't been real account-ability, ability to speak up to senior leadership, or transparency about key aspects of the business. Ultimately, the company lost their clients' trust and went bankrupt.

Are We as Values-Driven and Ethical as We Think?

Just as organizations will often claim adherence to noble values and assume that they have a healthy culture, leaders are equally inclined to assume that they're values-driven. When faced with a values dilemma, there is a tendency to assume we would make the right decision. We would speak up. We would deal with unhelpful or destructive behavior. We would not make unethical decisions for selfish reasons. We would leave the toxic culture.

However, we are often less values-driven
and ethical than we assume.

Imagine gathering a group of leaders in a room and asking them to rate themselves on different abilities. For example, how good they are at negotiating, making decisions, or being honest. Participants are instructed to give themselves any grade on a scale from zero to one hundred. However, they're told that fifty means they see their ability as equal to the group average. What do you think would happen? Renowned business ethics professor Ann Tenbrunsel, coauthor of *Blind Spots*, performed this experiment numerous times with hundreds of participants. When she divided the total grades by the number of participants, they should have added up to fifty. Yet they rarely did. The participants had positive illusions and graded themselves above average on abilities such as negotiating and decision-making. However, they had hyperillusions and rated themselves far above average on abilities related to how ethical or honest they are.[5]

Overestimating our values-driven nature and our ability to make good and ethical decisions can lead us to deviate from the right course and make poor decisions with significant negative consequences. Warning examples abound.

Three Ways We Lose Sight of Our Values

When I left the destructive community and gradually realized what a toxic environment I had been a part of and how blind I had been, I thought it was just me and that few people would be able to relate to my experience. However, after spending the last several years working with hundreds of leaders across several countries, I've concluded that I'm not alone.

> *While the situation and the degree of dysfunction and toxicity differs, I've found that all leaders are susceptible to personal blind spots and cultural pressures.*

Therefore, we will take a look at three ways we might lose sight of our values. The four culture-building habits and twelve practices will then help us avoid these pitfalls.

1. We lose sight of values when framing decisions.

While I've always wanted this book to be helpful to readers, I must admit that a selfish motive behind spending countless hours researching culture and human behavior has been to answer my own deepest questions. For example, I've wanted to comprehend how it was possible for us, as members of the destructive cult, to lose sight of fundamental values such as love, kindness, and respect in our actions and decision-making (values that are supposed to be central tenets of the Christian faith we professed). I found an answer in an interview I did with Professor Ann Tenbrunsel in November 2020.

Tenbrunsel and her colleague David Messick discovered a fascinating phenomenon in their research. As we approach a decision, we quickly assess what type of decision it is and what parameters should be considered. It helps us save time and avoid having to consider every possible variable. We might, for example, frame it as merely a legal decision or financial decision. (In my context, decisions were often framed as faith-based or spiritual decisions.) However, by putting the decision into a specific frame, we might subconsciously conclude that it's not a values-related decision. They called this phenomenon "ethical fading."[6]

We can see ethical fading at work in some of the most famous corporate scandals. Like the emissions scandal at Volkswagen, where decision-makers prioritized business goals over environmental standards and framed the decision to install software in diesel engines to cheat on emissions tests as merely an "engineering decision."[7] Or the Ford Pinto scandal, where treating a vital car manufacturing decision as merely a cost-benefit analysis led the Ford team to disregard crash tests showing that the fuel tank design was prone to catching fire in rear-end collisions, because "an analysis suggested it would be cheaper to pay off lawsuits than make the $11-per-vehicle fix."[8] The decision resulted in several fatal accidents and a very costly scandal for the company.

Tenbrunsel told me, "Your values and principles are important, but they will not serve as an impermeable buffer against unethical behavior. If you don't see the decision as an ethical decision, those values and principles simply won't make it into your decision."[9]

Our values and ethical principles are shoved aside and rendered useless as we silently move them out of our decision-making processes.

2. We compromise on our values because we want to fit in.

The main reason why I didn't speak up or take a stand, as a member of the destructive community, was fear. I wanted to fit in. I wanted to be accepted. I didn't want to be the odd one out. I wanted to be seen as successful and celebrated within the group.

Group pressure is a common way we lose sight of our values and fall into blindness. You've probably experienced it too. Imagine for a moment that the fire alarm goes off in your office. Instead of quickly heading to the emergency exits, you first look around to see how people around you react. If they continue to talk casually and act like nothing has happened, chances are you'll do the same, even though your life might be in danger. Many leaders have told me how certain behaviors, which they now in hindsight find unacceptable and in conflict with their values, were just the "way things were done" in their previous workplace or industry. They now can't understand how they compromised their values, but in that moment, they just wanted to fit in. Over time, they gradually became accustomed to the culture in their environment.

3. We accept a bad culture because of our noble mission.

But we have such an important mission, and we're doing so much good. This rationalization would often be my resort when the inner dissonance and moral turmoil became too loud to ignore. *Yes, we have things we need to work on, but the consequences of stopping now would be too great,* I would tell myself. I've heard similar reasoning numerous times from other leaders whether in large nonprofits driven by a world-changing vision, multinational medical technology companies selling lifesaving products, public organizations with a societal purpose, or other organizations that identify with having a noble mission. The assumption is that since we believe we are doing a lot of good, we can give ourselves license to do or at least tolerate some dysfunction and bad behavior. When team members voice concerns, leaders often point to the organization's positive impact as evidence that all is well, disregarding signs of a burgeoning toxic culture that, like a cancer, is silently eroding the organization from the inside.

I could go on and list numerous other ways we become blind, fall into tunnel vision, and lose sight of our values. However, these three examples are enough to highlight why staying true to our values is often harder than we might assume.

Personally, I truly want to be a values-driven leader, deliver great results, build a thriving workplace, and leave a positive legacy. I want to avoid experiencing the same regrets from my past.

> *I've realized that it takes consistent and intentional work and practice to live by the values I want to stand for and avoid tunnel vision and pitfalls.*

I can't just take it for granted, and the same holds true for you.

Before we move on to the habits and practices, let's prepare by exploring how you can best plan your journey to effectively grow your leadership and transform your workplace.

3

Planning Your Culture and Leadership Journey

We are what we repeatedly do.[1]

—Writer Will Durant's famous interpretation
of the words of Aristotle

M y wife was five months pregnant with our son in 2018 when a physiotherapist told me to refrain from carrying anything remotely heavy. I should not run, ride a bike (the most common mode of transportation in our city), or get on an airplane. The reason was a back problem that had given me growing discomfort and a wobbling sensation in my right leg. On top of the back issues, I lacked energy, had gained several unnecessary pounds, and looked out of shape.

That was when my wife gave me a gift—ten sessions with a personal trainer, marking the beginning of my transformational fitness journey. Even though I had only been exercising and caring about my health sporadically in the past, I now started forming new, healthier habits. The back issues gradually disappeared, and at the age of forty, I became stronger and fitter than ever before. My identity changed from thinking of myself as incapable of keeping a training habit to feeling uncomfortable when away from the gym for more than two days.

I'm sure we have all experienced the benefits and the pride of developing a new healthy habit and overcoming an unhealthy one. Even seemingly insignificant daily habits, such as flossing our teeth, leaving our phone off for an hour, spending a few minutes in quiet reflection before beginning the day, sharing a meal with family or friends, or starting our workday with a high-priority task, can lead to significant changes and give us a great sense of personal accomplishment. At the same time, we know how difficult it can be to sustain these habits and how easily we get off track when the inspiration wears off.

Overcoming Bad Leadership Habits

One of my proudest moments as a leader was when a team member said that they had never experienced working in an environment where concerns and contrary opinions were so intentionally welcomed and well received. I don't say this to brag, far from it. It brought me joy because I have failed so badly at it in the past (and still do at times).

Coming out of a toxic culture, I knew I didn't want to exhibit the elements of destructive leadership I had seen modeled. Despite that, I had unconsciously integrated some of these destructive elements and bad habits, along with my personal issues and insecurities, into my own leadership. I didn't handle opposing ideas well. I overreacted when team members failed at tasks that I deemed critical. I judged people without understanding what they were going through. I wanted loyalty to my mission and didn't comprehend that some people would flourish better in a different environment. I used my verbal skills to defeat others, taking pride in "winning" arguments. I later realized the need to make amends and have reached out to former team members to apologize for how these negative aspects of my leadership affected them.

However, somewhere along my leadership journey, by studying and learning from other leaders and mentors, growing in self-awareness and insight into culture, and being willing to get humble about my weaknesses and failures, I began to develop new habits and practices. I learned to take ownership and not look for scapegoats. I learned to solicit feedback and not assume people automatically felt safe to raise concerns with me. I learned to better recognize and celebrate my team members' contributions. I learned healthier ways to keep people accountable—practices and habits you'll learn more about in this book.

While I'm far from perfect on any of these things, the four culture-building habits and twelve practices in this book have had a profound impact on my personal leadership.

Witnessing their positive effects on so many other leaders we've worked with is amazing, and I can't wait to see how they will transform your leadership as well. As the title of this book suggests, you can culture!

Planning Your Journey

"You do not rise to the level of your goals. You fall to the level of your systems," wrote author James Clear in his insightful book *Atomic Habits*.[2]

I wrote this book to help you successfully develop the four critical culture-building habits and see real transformation in your team and organization. That's a big and bold ask, but I believe it's a worthwhile and attainable pursuit.

If you read this book like a regular book, I'm convinced it will be a game changer in your leadership.

However, truly developing and sustaining these habits might take some time. That's why I've designed an alternative journey through the book based on The Culture and Leadership Program, our company's high-impact leadership development and culture change program. Using the structure outlined below, you will be well equipped to make these new habits stick, grow your leadership and transform your cultural health.

1   **Know your why.**
    Developing and sustaining new habits takes commitment and consistency over time. That's why knowing your *why* is critical.

2 Take the journey over twelve months.

They say it takes twenty-one days to form a new habit.
However, a 2009 study in the *European Journal of Social
Psychology* showed that it varied between 18 and 254 days,
but the average was around two months.[3] That's why I
suggest spending three months on each culture-building
habit, focusing on one related practice every month. If, for
example, you prefer to take the journey over one calendar
year, your journey might look something like this (however,
you may extend it, allowing breaks for holidays):

January	**Habit 1:** **Get Humble**	**Practice 1:** Embrace Vulnerability
February		**Practice 2:** Take Ownership and Action
March		**Practice 3:** Restore Broken Trust
April	**Habit 2:** **Get Clear**	**Practice 4:** Make Values Matter
May		**Practice 5:** Celebrate the Right Behaviors
June		**Practice 6:** Deal with Unhelpful or Destructive Behavior
July	**Habit 3:** **Get Listening**	**Practice 7:** Solicit Feedback and Break the Silence
August		**Practice 8:** Create Conditions for Brave Conversations
September		**Practice 9:** Exercise Voicing Values
October	**Habit 4:** **Get Integrity**	**Practice 10:** Share Stories That Embody Mission and Values
November		**Practice 11:** Design Culture-Building Rituals
December		**Practice 12:** Rethink Incentives and Processes for Cultural Health

3   **Embark on the journey as a community.**

We're often the most successful with developing habits when we have the support and accountability of a group of trusted peers. While taking the journey on your own will give you great value, I encourage you to, if possible, take it together with others. Research on transfer of training shows that much of actual learning and development happens not in formal learning but in social/collaborative learning settings and on-the-job experiences.

In The Culture and Leadership Program, we combine individual learning with social learning in large workshops and peer group learning in small "growth groups" of four to five peers from within the organization. The growth groups gather monthly to reflect on the content, share their learnings and challenges, and hold one another accountable for their growth.

I encourage you to put together your growth group and meet monthly to reflect on what you've been reading and learning. It might be a group of managers or executives in your organization, or a group of leaders and friends from other organizations. You will discover reflections and actions at the end of each practice that are well suited for both individual and group reflection and growth.

Go to youcanculture.com for video resources and sample agendas for your growth group meetings.

4 Be sensitive to cultural nuances.

I've had the privilege of working with organizations and teams across several continents and in diverse cultural contexts. However, being born in Sweden and having spent most of my time in Europe and the US, I naturally tend to understand the world through that cultural lens. While I'm convinced these habits and practices are universally relevant, whether in India, the US, Germany, Nigeria, the UK, or Brazil, you will, of course, need to be sensitive to your cultural context in how you tactically apply them. If you are, for example, a part of a multinational growth group, having respectful conversations about how that application might differ can promote cross-cultural understanding.

5 **Allocate time for reading, reflection, and action.**
Creating new culture-building habits takes time, and it will require prioritization even when other things seem more urgent. However, it can save you much time that you might otherwise spend on dealing with division, disengagement, distrust, and dysfunction.

I suggest making room for the following time commitments each month:

- Individual learning: Set aside about thirty minutes monthly to read through one practice and reflect on the related questions.
- Peer learning: Schedule seventy-five minutes monthly for reflection with your growth group.
- On-the-job action: Work intentionally on implementing that practice's point of action in your day-to-day leadership.

6 **Assess results at the end of the year.**
As I mentioned in chapter 1, you're never done with improving culture or growing your leadership. However, the end of year one would be a great time to stop, assess, and celebrate the wins. What has changed in your leadership? What has changed in your team or organization? I would love to hear your stories of transformation. You can submit them on youcanculture.com.

Let's Begin Your Journey

You're now done preparing. You've reflected on the meaning of culture, clarified your why, dispelled myths, and mapped out a plan for your journey. Now it's time to start the journey of transforming your cultural health! As we start with Habit 1: Get Humble, I'm cheering you on. While it might seem counterintuitive, there's a good reason why I chose to start the journey with getting humble—it's the culture-building habit that will unlock the three other habits.

Let's get started, and remember, you can culture!

Habit 1

Get Humble

Do you wish to rise? Begin by descending.
You plan a tower that will pierce the clouds?
Lay first the foundation of humility.[1]

—Augustine of Hippo

4

Missed Warnings, a Scandal, and the Call for Humility

It was a bitterly cold morning. An ice storm gripped parts of the American Midwest. I remember being hit by a cold gust of wind as I raced between the warmth of my hotel and the safety of my rental car. I had flown in from Sweden, invited by the interim executive team at a well-regarded nonprofit. This organization, once lauded by a distinguished workplace institute as being a great place to work with an excellent culture, was now navigating the devastating ramifications of a crisis.

The well-respected founder, internationally known as a bestselling author and leadership icon, was caught up in serious allegations of sexual improprieties and misuse of power. The allegations, which had been brought to the attention of the board of directors years earlier by a group of former leaders and team members, had been dismissed, as the board sided with the founder's version of events. However, the story didn't end there. When the Me Too movement spread like wildfire in 2017–2018 and uncovered abuse, harassment, and toxicity in countless organizations, a whistleblower brought the allegations to a major newspaper. As the story broke, the founder and the board contended that it was a coordinated effort to destroy the founder's reputation. As the pressure grew and new information materialized, the founder, nearing retirement, decided to step aside. Ultimately, the entire board resigned, having initiated an independent investigation that found that the sexual misconduct allegations were credible and that their culture had contributed to a negative use of power, influence, and management style. An interim executive team had been put in the unenviable position of restoring trust, addressing cultural challenges, and dealing with significant reputational and financial damage.

The message I gave the executive team reflects my frequent advice to organizations facing crises or urgent cultural challenges: The urge to move on as quickly as possible, to shift the focus away from the past and get busy with the mission and move forward with a new strategy can be tempting, but risks having severe long-term effects if the root causes aren't addressed. And while improving governance and compliance structures would be critical, to try to avoid similar misconduct, such actions alone wouldn't sufficiently address the underlying cultural challenges.

The leadership needed to acknowledge that their response to the allegations and the resulting situation had revealed a significant lack of cultural health that shouldn't be brushed aside. That they had been more concerned with protecting their reputation than maintaining integrity around their values. They had been more protective of their brand than their cultural health. Their focus on their legacy had taken precedence over addressing the welfare of the people in their care. They had bought into the health illusion and the bad apple myth—assumed that they were healthy and tried to frame their accusers as bad apples—which had led them to overlook red flags and fight relevant concerns instead of addressing them.

However, there was an opportunity for them to come out of this crisis in a healthier state, more adept at facing whatever challenges may lie ahead. They had the potential to rebuild and even strengthen trust with those people who invested so much in their mission. While vulnerability might be unsettling and uncomfortable, pride and willful blindness would be much more dangerous in the long run. The first thing they needed to do to transform their cultural health was to get humble.

A Radical Response to Cultural Challenges

While few of us find ourselves in a situation like the one I just described, we will all encounter instances where we fail in our leadership, face cultural challenges, and drift off from the mission and values we claim. For many organizations, it manifests in issues such as division, distrust, silence, disengagement, dysfunction, and attrition—issues that will negatively affect our ability to deliver on our mission, retain great talent, and get the best ideas on the table. Issues that are much easier to address in their infancy than when they have become entrenched.

Getting humble helps us quickly identify signs of issues in our leadership or culture and respond effectively.

Instead of becoming defensive and protective, which only exacerbates the problems, we take ownership and action, and we do the work needed to repair broken trust. It's impossible to sustain cultural health and values-driven leadership without the willingness to get humble. While it might initially feel like showing weakness, you will find that it is, in fact, showing true leadership courage and strength.

The Habit at a Glance

As leaders, we will, at times, realize that we have acted in conflict with our mission or values, become a part of hindering behavioral patterns, or begun to accept a lack of cultural health. When these issues are hidden, disregarded, or not dealt with consistently and urgently, there is a risk of breaking trust and impairing our ability to fulfill the mission, build a thriving workplace, and have a responsible impact. However, by embracing vulnerability, taking ownership, and actively working to repair broken trust, we can avoid pitfalls and transform our cultural health.

Practices to Get Humble

In this quarter, we will explore three monthly practices designed to help you get humble.

Practice 1: Embrace Vulnerability

To avoid willful blindness and the effects of a lack of cultural health, we shouldn't assume that our culture is healthy; instead, openly admit that we are vulnerable and have the potential to veer off course from our mission and values, even with good intentions. Embracing vulnerability and admitting our challenges and mistakes strengthens trust and a culture of learning.

Practice 2: Take Ownership

Culture is always cocreated. To transform our cultural health, we must stop blaming others and recognize how we, as leaders, have contributed to the cultural challenges at hand. When we take ownership, focus on what we can control or influence, and begin to change the behaviors we model, encourage, or condone, we can inspire change and build trust and commitment with the people we lead.

Practice 3: Repair Broken Trust

When we've failed to act in line with our mission and values, overlooked cultural challenges, or caused harm, we need to repair broken trust and our cultural health by (1) acknowledging the harm we've contributed to and offering a sincere apology, (2) explaining what went wrong, and (3) clarifying how we will act differently in the future. Even if the fault is not directly ours, addressing the issue is our responsibility.

5

Practice 1:
Embrace Vulnerability

It seemed like just another research assignment. Lenny Wong, now a retired research professor at the US Army War College, was tasked by the chief of staff to study why junior officers exhibited less innovation, creativity, and independent thinking. Wong traveled worldwide with a task force and interviewed army staff to understand the issue. What he found surprised him. The army had burdened junior leaders with so many demands and requirements that they spent almost all their time doing what someone else had told them to do—take mandatory training. While they only had 256 available training days, they had 297 days of required training. Obviously, there was little time for independent thinking or innovation.

Wong concluded the study and reported back the results. However, he was left with an uncomfortable question: If the army requires more from officers than they can literally and physically accomplish, then what are they reporting? Deep down, Wong knew the answer. In the army, you must report that you're getting everything done. Otherwise, you would have to look for another profession. There was only one answer: they were not telling the truth—a severe values conflict in a profession that prides itself on officers' words as their bond.

In most cases, this is where the story would end since no one would volunteer to challenge such a sacred assumption. It would be much easier to stay in the comfort of the health illusion. However, several years after ending the study, Wong sat down with his research partner, Stephen Gerras, and said,

"I think I've got an idea for another study.
I think we should talk about how we lie."[1]

As they began the study, they found more examples of this systemic dishonesty. Wong told me that in the army, they were focused on leadership development. An important part of it is quarterly evaluations, where the rating officer sits down with subordinates to rate their progress on goals and responsibilities. The problem is that they are often in different parts of the world or too busy to make the meeting happen. Yet the officer has to input the date the meeting occurred into a system. Without the option to select that it didn't happen, officers would routinely choose an arbitrary date. These might appear like trivial issues, yet Wong found that a culture of dishonesty creates a moral numbness and a slippery slope. He interviewed a colonel assigned to inspect 150 polling sites in Iraq before the elections to ensure their security. The colonel told Wong that it was physically impossible to get it all done, yet he had been given a spreadsheet that his superiors expected him to complete. "I just gave them what they wanted," the colonel told Wong.

When the study was published, the reactions varied. Douglas Lovelace, director of the Strategic Studies Institute at the US Army War College, wrote in his foreword, "Discussing dishonesty in the army profession is a topic that will undoubtedly make many readers uneasy. It is, however, a concern that must be addressed to better the Army profession."[2] At junior levels, people said, "This is nothing new. We see this every day." However, at senior levels, Wong said, there was a tendency to think, "Well, let's not talk about it." As stewards of the profession, leaders didn't want to admit that there was truth to the study findings.

What fascinates me is that the cultural issues weren't uncovered by outsiders (which could have led to a scandal) but by people inside the army who chose to notice and ask hard and uncomfortable questions. Instead of orchestrating a cover-up, they decided to dig deeper and care about the cultural health. They did it openly and transparently, inviting the whole profession to learn, ultimately leading to important changes.

Wong told me in a 2020 interview that organizations want to aspire to the highest values. "We don't want to say that we accept less-than-perfect values, and yet we have to balance that with, as individuals, as humans, we're not perfect." He believed we must ensure that we don't create a culture where people are compelled to lie to maintain the appearance of a perfect organization. Instead of trying to appear spotless, we must embrace vulnerability.

Strengthening Trust through an "Assume Breach" Mentality

Does a 100 percent secure IT network or system exist? Of course not. They all have vulnerabilities. A leading network security website suggested that IT managers should have an "assume breach" mentality, noting, "Given that a certain amount of risk of breach is inevitable on all practical systems, it is safer to defend your systems with this attitude."[3] If we assume the system is vulnerable to attacks and breaches, we will make regular tests since it's better to identify those vulnerabilities ourselves than to fall prey to external hackers or malware.

We must adopt a similar "assume breach" mentality when it comes to our leadership and the culture within our team or organization. It is the only way to avoid falling prey to the health illusion—assuming our culture is healthy without conducting a true assessment of the reality.

However, I have spoken to many leaders who feared that admitting vulnerabilities risked disregarding all the great things about their leadership, culture, and organization. It doesn't. While our leadership and culture will have many admirable qualities, there will still be issues and vulnerabilities. Embracing vulnerability and acknowledging flaws and challenges is not a sign of weakness; rather, it reflects honesty and authenticity and ultimately makes us stronger (and it's likely that our team members have long since noticed the issues).

We trust and admire leaders and team members who can be honest and vulnerable about not only their successes but also their shortcomings and failures. Who can give a more meaningful answer when talking about their weaknesses than the fictional Michael Scott in the sitcom *The Office*: "I work too hard, I care too much, and sometimes I can be too invested in my job."

Jeffrey Polzer, a professor of organizational behavior at Harvard whose research is focused on how people collaborate in teams, told author Daniel Coyle in *The Culture Code*, "People tend to think of vulnerability in a touchy-feely way, but that's not what's happening.

It's about sending a really clear signal that you have weaknesses, that you could use help. And if that behavior becomes a model for others, then you can set the insecurities aside and get to work, start to trust each other, and help each other. If you never have that vulnerable moment, on the other hand, then people will try to cover up their weaknesses, and every little microtask becomes a place where insecurities manifest themselves."[4]

Without acknowledging our vulnerabilities, faults, and mistakes, we won't learn to do better. We won't grow in our leadership, and we will be more susceptible to overlooking critical red flags.

The Significance of Embracing Vulnerability

Some time ago, I worked with an executive team where a few members were unwilling to admit mistakes and entertain the possibility that they were wrong. It caused a lot of frustration and division and made it hard for them to move forward on solving real issues, which had adverse effects that could have been largely avoidable. It also caused a lack of vulnerability, learning, and courage among middle and frontline managers. Ultimately, two people had to be moved off the team for them to finally be able to move forward.

In Practice 7, we'll explore how to actively solicit feedback and invite people to show where you might be wrong and what blind spots you might be unaware of. However, this first practice begins with a shift of mindset. You are vulnerable. You have flaws. You have blind spots. You can lose sight of your values. While I'm sure you would never end up in the kind of destructive culture and unethical decisions I did, you can end up with tunnel vision too. You can make a wrong decision even if you have good intentions. The same is true of your organization.

As organizational psychologist Adam Grant wrote in *Think Again*, "Humility is often misunderstood. It's not a matter of having low self-confidence. One of the Latin roots of humility means 'from the earth.' It's about being grounded—recognizing that we're flawed and fallible."[5]

Being Quick to Course Correct

Several years ago, I was out canoeing with my twelve-year-old daughter in the canals that stretch throughout our city of Malmö, Sweden. She wanted to sit in the back of the canoe and hence be in charge of direction. However, we quickly began to paddle in a peculiar pattern. We zigzagged from one side to the other, finding ourselves stuck repeatedly and spending more time untangling the canoe from branches and bushes than making progress. If you have some experience canoeing, you know that to paddle effectively, the last thing you should do is focus on avoiding the banks. If you only react when you're dangerously close to hitting a tree, it will often be too late to course correct—especially if you are inexperienced. Instead, you need to focus on staying centered and making course corrections as soon as you start drifting off.

Often, as leaders and organizations, we tend to take far too long to correct course: disregarding and making excuses for a team member or leader who continually shows proof of bad or toxic behavior; accepting the little feedback we get in team meetings, even though we know there are many opinions that aren't being shared; overlooking tensions between department heads that have begun to seep into the whole organization; disregarding the fact that our current culture doesn't support key elements of our strategy. The list goes on.

> *However, the longer it takes to*
> *acknowledge and diagnose the issue,*
> *the more entrenched the problem becomes.*

We find ourselves caught in the banks and lose momentum. We are forced to spend valuable time and resources fixing issues that could have been avoided.

If, instead, we focus on the center—on building remarkable cultural health and maintaining alignment with our mission, strategy, and values—while continually inviting feedback to help us see where we're getting offtrack, admitting failures, and making minor adjustments, we will be much more likely to remain centered and successfully reach our destination. Embracing vulnerability helps us quickly make these course corrections because we are ready to listen, learn, and seek out critical information.

Five Ways We Can Embrace Vulnerability

What does it practically entail to embrace vulnerability? Here are five things we can all do:

1 **Take signals seriously.**
   Take bad behavior, lack of integrity, or a lack of cultural health seriously, whether brought to your attention by external or internal sources. While you should never uncritically believe the information, decide to dig deeper and

listen instead of trying to cover it up. Don't assume that this couldn't be happening in your leadership, team, or organization; assume that it could.

2   Communicate your values with humility.

Avoid communicating statements such as "Our corporate values guide all our behavior and permeate our culture" or "We are a corruption-free organization." While these ideals may be your ongoing pursuit, have the humility to acknowledge that they are by no means guaranteed.

One of our clients formulated their stance on their values this way: "Our values help us ask the right questions about how we should lead, act, and conduct our business. However, it is in the way we actually think, work, and make decisions that the truth of what we value is revealed. Our espoused values and behaviors are a description of our aspiration, not in all respects a representation of our current reality. Our values must therefore drive us to consistently work on being a genuinely values-driven organization."

3   Acknowledge the ways in which you've failed.

I've shared my story of becoming complicit in a destructive culture with thousands of leaders. While it can still be scary and emotional, I've learned that sharing examples of my failures while taking ownership of my actions gives others permission to get humble and be vulnerable too.

We all have different experiences and failures, and sharing them can empower our team members and peers to embrace their vulnerabilities as well. However, it needs to happen within healthy boundaries so that we're not creating confusion or burdening people with issues they aren't supposed to carry. As Brené Brown, bestselling researcher on courage, vulnerability, and shame, wrote in *Daring Greatly*, "Vulnerability is based on mutuality and requires boundaries and trust. It's not oversharing."[6]

Sharing the right kind of information in a safe environment with your team or peers will inspire courage in others.

While you keep talking about all the great things happening in your organization, instill the mindset, from the CEO to the front line, that you embrace vulnerability and will never take cultural health for granted.

4 Ask for help.

One of the hardest things I know is asking for help. Not necessarily help to complete a task—although that might sometimes be challenging as well—but help because I'm struggling in my leadership or in my personal life. And so often, after I finally take the courage to ask someone for help, I will, in hindsight, wish I would have made that decision much sooner.

I've seen numerous cultural challenges with significant consequences that could have been averted if the manager or executive in charge had simply asked for help. Often, a simple consultation with their superior or a peer would have sufficed. In more complex situations, it would have been wise to turn to HR or ethics and compliance or get outside counsel. It's not about dumping the issue onto someone else but rather about inviting diverse perspectives and insights.

In asking for help, we practice humility and embrace vulnerability. It's astonishing how willing people are to assist and how much we can learn from the people around us.

5 Make reflecting on your values and leadership a ritual.

There are many reasons why we easily lose sight of our values, even though we want to assume that we're values-driven (as we explored in chapter 2). Regularly engaging in self-reflection regarding our leadership and personal and organizational values—identifying priorities, decision-making foundations, and nonnegotiables—helps us make better decisions and avoid succumbing to ethical tunnel vision and willful blindness. The key, however, lies in turning such reflection into a ritual.

For me, it involves an early morning routine of reading, reflecting, and journaling and having people in my life with whom I regularly engage in intentional conversations about values and priorities and who know the truth about me, flaws and all. When I neglect these practices, I find that I slowly drift away from my professed values. I begin to believe I'm invincible, and I risk losing the essential guardrails that protect me from my worst instincts.

Through my work with clients, I've encountered various approaches to incorporating reflective time into one's routine. For instance, an executive made a habit of driving home from work without taking calls or turning on the radio to give himself the time to ask, *What kind of influence has my leadership had on other people today?* Or another manager who blocked off ten minutes in her calendar each week to journal and reflect on whether she had aligned her actions with her values that week.

The key is to find a ritual or practice that suits your life situation. However, I can promise that implementing this ritual will improve your leadership. You will become better at standing up for your values and have a more positive influence on your team and culture.

You Can Culture   Month 1

Reflect

- What is your gut reaction when people raise concerns or issues regarding your leadership or the culture within your team and organization?
- Reflecting on past experiences, where have you struggled to acknowledge real issues?
- Are there areas where you might be hesitant or unwilling to acknowledge current concerns?

Act

- Commit to a regular ritual (daily or a few times a week) to intentionally reflect on your/your organization's values and the impact of your leadership, both positive and negative. Consider the changes and challenges you observe over time.

The Practice at a Glance

To avoid willful blindness and the effects of a lack of cultural health, we shouldn't assume that our culture is healthy; instead, openly admit that we are vulnerable and have the potential to veer off course from our mission and values, even with good intentions. Embracing vulnerability and admitting our challenges and mistakes strengthens trust and a culture of learning.

" While our leadership and culture will have many admirable qualities, there will still be issues and vulnerabilities.

Embracing vulnerability and acknowledging flaws and challenges is not a sign of weakness; rather, it reflects honesty and authenticity and ultimately makes us stronger. "

Further Resources

Books:

- *Blind Spots: Why We Fail to Do What's Right and What to Do about It* by Ann E. Tenbrunsel and Max H. Bazerman
- *Think Again: The Power of Knowing What You Don't Know* by Adam Grant
- *Dare to Lead: Brave Work. Tough Conversations. Whole Hearts.* by Brené Brown

Podcasts:

- "Are We as Ethical as We Think?"—my interview with Ann Tenbrunsel on the *Leading Transformational Change* podcast
- "Uncovering a Culture of Dishonesty"—my interview with Lenny Wong on the *Leading Transformational Change* podcast

VISIT **YOUCANCULTURE.COM**
FOR MORE RESOURCES.

6

Practice 2:
Take Ownership and Action

I t looked like a reputational catastrophe. On April 16, 2006, Greenpeace activists dressed up as giant chickens protested in McDonald's restaurants around the United Kingdom, holding large yellow signs with the message "Stop trashing the Amazon for fast food."[1] Some activists even chained themselves to chairs, causing a lot of commotion and drawing international publicity.

Greenpeace claimed that the large-scale production of soy, fed to chickens that end up in McNuggets, led to severe deforestation in the Amazon. This was a surprise for Bob Langert, vice president of corporate social responsibility and sustainability at McDonald's. He contacted a few experts to vet the accuracy of the data and found that it was fundamentally true. However, he learned that McDonald's supply chain accounted for less than 0.5 percent of all soy purchased. Langert told me in a 2021 interview that he, together with other leaders in Supply Chain and Public Affairs, decided not to debate Greenpeace. Instead they decided, in conflict with the typical corporate instincts, to take ownership and test the waters to see if Greenpeace would engage in a dialogue so that they, together, could play a role in driving change. And they did. Within twenty-four hours, a team at McDonald's approached Greenpeace to acknowledge the problem and ask to partner up. While they alone couldn't change the soy industry overnight, they were ready to get to work. Langert and colleagues traveled with Greenpeace to the Amazon rainforest and learned more about the issue of deforestation. Together, they got the major suppliers to the table and leveraged them to implement important changes. Researchers have found that the initiative "helped to drastically reduce the amount of deforestation linked to soy production in the region."[2]

This idea of listening to critics and acknowledging responsibility, however, hadn't come naturally to McDonald's. Their historical response had typically been to defend the notion that they were a good organization with good values and either ignore the critics or take them on. Over time, however, they realized their approach was far from constructive. Langert and his team began to see ominous signs that while the company continued to grow, trust in the brand had deteriorated because of the lack of focus on ethics and sustainability.

Langert told me his new modus operandi involved researching and acknowledging the issues raised and finding partners for collaboration. It could even go as far as inviting their critics into the restaurant kitchens and getting their insights on implementing more sustainable practices within their current business model. He added that his main regret was that they didn't proactively start taking ownership soon enough. He believed tackling the issues head-on instead of waiting for someone to point them out would have enabled them to be more of a force for positive change. Langert said that "for your organization to get credit for the 80 percent you are doing good, you need to take ownership of and admit the 20 percent where you're not succeeding."[3] Customers understand that you aren't perfect, but they want to know that you are humble, ready to take ownership and action.

Identifying Your Role

When we are alerted, whether through internal or external sources, to ways we are acting in conflict with our values, the temptation is always there to start pointing the finger at everyone else.

In the case of McDonald's, a well-worn defense would be that everyone else is doing it and that it's unfair to blame one company—a strategy that would result in inertia and inaction.

Similarly, when we see symptoms of cultural challenges within our team or organization, we are tempted to merely point at team members or external actors whom we believe are the source of the dysfunction while disregarding our role as leaders. However, blaming a few bad apples is not an effective response, and it makes us overlook possible broader issues within our leadership or culture that do need to be addressed. Let's look at two examples that might hit even closer to home.

Example 1: A Toxic Culture and Complicit Managers

An organization identified elements of disrespectful behavior in several teams. They assumed the problem was just a few team members behaving badly. However, when we interviewed team members and assessed the culture within the organization, it became clear that some managers were partaking in the disrespectful behavior and the coarse jokes, either directly by being in on the jokes or indirectly by not speaking up about the behavior. This gave the perception that the behavior was tolerated or even encouraged by some managers.

Example 2: An Executive Who Mistrusted His Team Members

A CEO was frustrated over his company's perceived lack of independent thinking, decision-making, and initiative, with concerns about the potential future impact on business performance. His diagnosis pointed to a fundamental problem: a hesitancy among employees to take bold actions. Communicating this concern to his team, he emphasized the need for improved initiative-taking and that he neither wanted nor could be involved in all business decisions.

However, a revealing pattern emerged during our cultural assessment. Although the CEO delegated responsibility for a specific project, claiming not to have time to be involved, he often intervened at the last minute, making major changes to his colleagues' decisions. Despite outwardly advocating for a hands-off approach and encouraging others to take the lead in decision-making, he inadvertently assumed the roles of both micromanager and chief decision-maker. Consequently, this relegated others to the role of mere implementers who wanted to ensure they had the CEO's explicit approval to avoid last-minute project alterations.

I encourage you to stop and take a moment to reflect on a cultural challenge you face, and identify the behavioral patterns at play by applying the culture as a dance performance metaphor discussed in chapter 1. (Similar to watching a dance performance and focusing our attention on an individual dancer's movements, disregarding the larger pattern and the diverse roles being played, we may be tempted to solely focus on the behavior of one or a few team members, overlooking the behavioral pattern and the roles we have taken on within it.) Now, reflect on the various roles at play in that behavioral pattern, identifying your own role, and consider how your actions might contribute to perpetuating the pattern through the behavior you model, encourage, incentivize, or tolerate.

REFLECTION

Can you identify the role you play? What impact could it have on the cultural pattern?

While it might seem difficult at first, looking at your cultural challenges through this lens will often lead to some eye-opening insights that could be the starting point of the change you need.

Blaming Bad Apples Leads to Silence

In 2015, a small group of researchers in a US-based lab found that Volkswagen engineers had installed "defeat devices" to cheat emissions tests on their diesel vehicles and that the emissions output could be up to forty-times higher than advertised. Volkswagen, famous for the efficient quality of their cars, was now being seen as a company of cheaters who, in their push for growth, had cut corners and were caught red-handed.

While it may appear that a few engineers caused the company's woes, the underlying issue ran much deeper. Hiltrud Werner, recruited to head up legal and integrity in the wake of the scandal as a member of the Volkswagen management board, told me in a 2020 interview that, "Employees and management wanted to believe that the problem was just a few bad apples and not an issue of corporate culture. There was this 'too big to fail' attitude. Why should we listen to the outside world? We are the benchmark. However, there was not enough openness to discuss their own behavior and not a culture of speaking up."[4]

As illustrated in the above example, blaming bad apples fails to acknowledge those who should have noticed but consciously chose not to see or to act, often because they had something to gain from remaining blind or silent. I discussed the Volkswagen case with Professor Margaret Heffernan, who has dedicated many years to researching and writing on the danger of willful blindness. She told me, "At first, everybody says, 'Oh, we couldn't possibly have known.' Then they say it's a few bad apples. Then it turns out that quite a lot of people knew, and then it turns out that kind of everybody knew or could have known."[5] Looking back at my personal story, it's clear that while the founder was ultimately responsible for shaping the destructive culture, it would be incorrect to disregard the willful blindness, silence, and complicity it required of the rest of us.

We had a responsibility to see and to act, even if it was convenient to claim the problem was solely someone else's.

Identifying Our Circles of Control and Influence

The above examples highlight the consequences of disregarding and not taking ownership of our role in the cultural challenges we face. However, they also present a possibility. By identifying our role and changing our behavior, we can contribute to change and transformation. In his classic bestseller *The 7 Habits of Highly Effective People*, Stephen Covey introduced a model he called the circle of influence/circle of concern.[6] I'll use a slightly modified version here with three circles instead of two.

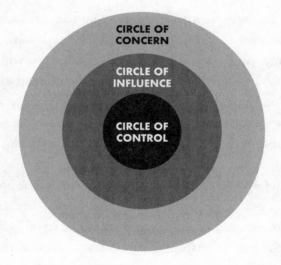

- The *circle of control* represents the things you have control over, such as your actions, attitudes, and responses. As the psychiatrist and Holocaust survivor Viktor Frankl wrote in *Man's Search for Meaning*, "The one thing you can't take away from me is the way I choose to respond to what you do to me. The last of one's freedoms is to choose one's attitude in any given circumstance."[7]

- The *circle of influence* represents the things we can't control but do have influence over. While you can't and shouldn't try to control your team, you do have the ability to influence them through your example, the vision you set, the stories you tell, and the behavior you encourage or choose to tolerate.

  Depending on your role within the organization, the number of things you can influence or have control over, of course, varies.

- The *circle of concern* represents things outside your control or influence that can still impact your organization, team, and your own situation. We could, for example, put market conditions and unforeseen global events, such as a pandemic, here. But depending on your role, your circle of concern might include the company's strategy, or an upcoming mass layoff that you have no influence over.

When I work with leadership development, I often go back to these three circles and implore leaders that while they shouldn't disregard their circle of concern, they should start by focusing on the things they can control or at least influence. I encourage you to do the same as you read this book. By focusing first on what you have the ability to control or influence, you will be much better positioned to help bring positive change.

Taking Ownership and Action
Can Change Everything

One of our clients, a utility company, saw a pressing need to address and transform two aspects of their culture for better alignment with their business strategy and to foster a healthier workplace. However, as my colleagues and I helped their executive team delve deeper into leadership behavior, processes, and incentives that needed to evolve to influence their culture positively, they got stuck in all the reasons why they couldn't alter their methods and incentive systems to strengthen collaboration or deal with inappropriate behavior from high performers. It felt like a dead end. While they claimed on the one hand that change was required, on the other hand, when push came to shove, they wanted to avoid doing the work.

Ultimately, I presented the CEO with a challenge. I asked her to reflect on her own role and consider aspects within her circle of control and influence that she was personally willing to change to improve the culture. I emphasized that to bring about any meaningful change, she would need to start by taking ownership and action, and then she could extend the same challenge to the rest of the executive leadership and, subsequently, to their managers. Only when every one of them had identified ways to contribute should they ask anything of the broader organization. She quickly decided to embrace the challenge, and the rest of the leadership followed suit.

I realized we had a breakthrough when one of the department heads shared that he had begun to proactively schedule meetings with other department leaders to ask how they experienced collaborating with his department and what his department could do to improve that experience—an exemplary demonstration of an ownership mindset. As the initiative progressed, they began to see a significant improvement in collaboration among key departments that had previously struggled to work together effectively.

> *Without a readiness to see, accept,*
> *and acknowledge our role, our efforts to*
> *influence our culture will become manipulative*
> *and inauthentic and ultimately fail.*

On the other hand, when we take ownership and action, we can build trust and commitment.

Jay Barney, professor of strategic management and coauthor of *The Secret of Culture Change*, has studied organizations that succeeded with culture transformation. Instead of initiating the change effort by merely discussing values or announcing a culture change initiative, he discovered that the most successful initiatives began with leaders taking bold and tangible actions that embodied the desired values and culture. He told me in a 2023 interview that "leaders engaged in activities that exemplified a new culture that was clearly different from the current culture, but they didn't actually announce that they were going to change culture."[8] Taking action forced them to commit to the change process, and it became an authentic story that spread throughout the organization.

Courageously taking ownership allows us to become proactive and exemplify the transformation. While we can't ultimately decide how others respond, we can control our own actions. We can take a step toward change. We can begin the journey. As Siobhan McHale wrote in *The Insider's Guide to Culture Change*, "Never underestimate your power to change the culture, simply by changing your behavior."[9]

Imagine the impact when everyone, from the C-suite to frontline workers, is willing to take ownership. Instead of evading accountability, we take our values seriously and are eager to commit to embodying the change we want to see. We don't shy away from responsibility, even when taking ownership might be uncomfortable or daunting.

Instead of coming up with all the reasons why the issue is everyone else's fault, we begin by asking ourselves, "What is my responsibility?"

You Can Culture   Month 2

Reflection

- Consider a specific area/element of your culture—attitudes or behavioral patterns—where you see a critical need for change.
- What role has your leadership played in the behaviors you have modeled, encouraged, or tolerated? (If you struggle to identify your role, ask your fellow leaders or team members, "How has my leadership contributed to these behavioral patterns?")
- How can you, by taking ownership and changing your behavior or integrating a new, positive behavior, actively contribute to the necessary change?

Action

- Commit to something specific you will do to take ownership, take action, and begin to change or integrate a new, positive behavior to change the culture. Start acting in line with that decision, and consider the changes and challenges you observe over time.

The Practice at a Glance

Culture is always cocreated. To transform our cultural health, we must stop blaming others and recognize how we, as leaders, have contributed to the cultural challenges at hand. When we take ownership, focus on what we can control or influence, and begin to change the behaviors we model, encourage, or condone, we can inspire change and build trust and commitment with the people we lead.

" *While we can't ultimately decide how others respond, we can control our own actions. We can take a step toward change. We can begin the journey.* "

Further Resources

Books:

- *The Insider's Guide to Culture Change: Creating a Workplace That Delivers, Grows, and Adapts* by Siobhan McHale
- *The Battle to Do Good: Inside McDonald's Sustainability Journey* by Bob Langert
- *The 7 Habits of Highly Effective People: Powerful Lessons in Personal Change* by Stephen R. Covey
- *Willful Blindness: Why We Ignore the Obvious at Our Peril* by Margaret Heffernan

Podcasts:

- "How Taking Ownership and Action Will Transform Your Culture"—my interview with Jay Barney on the *Leading Transformational Change* podcast
- "A Guide to Culture Change in a Time of Crisis"—my interview with Siobhan McHale on the *Leading Transformational Change* podcast
- "Mapping the Future and Avoiding Wilful Blindness"—my interview with Margaret Heffernan on the *Leading Transformational Change* podcast
- "Collaborating with Your Toughest Critics"—my interview with Bob Langert on the *Leading Transformational Change* podcast

VISIT **YOUCANCULTURE.COM**
FOR MORE RESOURCES.

7

Practice 3:
Repair Broken Trust

I t was a make-it-or-break-it moment. The executive team and the board entered the stage to address hundreds of team members gathered in a large auditorium on a cold December day. The atmosphere was filled with tense anticipation, and you could hear a pin drop.

The chief executive took the mic to address the audience. She spoke with gratitude about the many incredible successes the organization had experienced in the past. She then shared about the change process they had begun. After a few minutes, she arrived at the part everyone had anxiously awaited. With a voice filled with conviction, she began:

"In our desire to promote a visionary and entrepreneurial type of leadership, which has been an important part of our historical success, we've created an unhealthy sense of respect for senior management, which has led to a destructive distance between leadership and staff. This has caused a special treatment of senior leaders, a fear of questioning superiors, a yes-sayer culture, and a lack of initiatives and innovation. As we move into the future, we want to build a culture of respect for each other, whatever role or function we hold, and be very intentional about avoiding any elements of fear or distance."

She then bravely addressed several other areas of the culture that had become unhealthy one by one. She followed a similar pattern—naming the problem, outlining the harm it had caused, and delving into the underlying beliefs, values, and drivers that had caused it. At the end of her speech, she and the leadership took ownership of the problems and apologized for the harm it had caused. They then detailed some significant cultural and structural changes they were committed to going forward with and how they would intentionally create a safe space for people to come and share their experiences and ask difficult questions. When they finished, they received a standing ovation.

> *It was a remarkable event because the chief executive and the executive team had mainly inherited the elements of a lack of cultural health from prior leadership, yet they took ownership.*

Additionally, it was remarkable because historically leaders in the organization had seldom apologized publicly for anything.

A few months before the event, the leadership had asked me to support them in addressing critical cultural challenges and a crisis of trust. They had undergone a complex leadership shift with significant complications. In the wake of the leadership transition, past missteps, abuse of power, a culture of silence, and other unhealthy and toxic elements of their culture surfaced. Some of the issues had been picked up by the media. The new senior leadership had initially tried to focus on the future and move on, but after some time, they realized that they had to address the lingering cultural challenges and the harm they had caused. This began a vulnerable and painful process that took significant courage and humility.

Apologizing in front of hundreds of people that day was not the end but the beginning of a transformative journey.

Over time, the broken trust was increasingly restored. Leaders and team members began to have hard conversations and raise concerns, confronting the culture of silence. A significant project, stalled because of the distrust and lack of financial commitment from donors, was launched. More and more evidence began to spread, indicating that something different was happening in the organization. The media wrote positive stories about the changes that had taken place. When the organization arranged an open leadership conference a few years later, hundreds of leaders gathered to hear the story of the remarkable turnaround that had reinvigorated an organization that many thought wouldn't be able to survive their crisis.

Trust Is a Vulnerable Relationship

Trust is business critical. No organization can be successful in the long term without the trust of its key stakeholders. Trust is an essential form of capital for every leader. We won't truly succeed as leaders or be able to cultivate cultural health without the trust of our team members.

Professor Sandra J. Sucher, an internationally recognized trust researcher at Harvard Business School, has found in her research that trust hinges on the fact that we are seen as:

1. competent to deliver,
2. having the right motives—authentically caring about doing right by others,
3. using fair means to achieve our goals, and
4. taking full responsibility for all the impacts of our actions.[1]

Yet, as we all know, trust is fragile and can easily be broken. As Sandra J. Sucher and journalist Shalene Gupta wrote in *The Power of Trust*,

> "To trust fundamentally means to make yourself vulnerable to the actions of others. We trust because we believe they will do right by us. When we choose to trust someone, we willingly give them power over us, trusting that they will not abuse this power. Trust is a special form of dependence and is predicated on the idea that we can be more than disappointed: we can be betrayed."[2]

Every time I read this quote, it makes me pause. I have, in both small and more consequential ways, failed to do right by people I've led. I've left people feeling disappointed and even betrayed. In some cases, it took me years until I reached out and apologized for the harm I had caused. I also know the disheartening feeling of being disappointed by leaders I've followed and admired. To realize that they weren't who they had claimed to be or that they acted unfairly and in ways that were contrary to the values they claimed to uphold. That lost trust could, however, have been repaired in most cases. What led to a sense of betrayal was realizing that they had no intention of owning up to the impact of their actions and that, at the end of the day, they cared more about their own self-interest and status than the mission and the well-being of the people they led.

Nevertheless, the majority of leaders I've encountered truly care about their mission and their team members. They are competent to get things done and aspire to operate fairly, guided by sound values. They care deeply about being seen as trustworthy. I'm sure that this is true about you as well.

However, as I emphasized in Practice 1, even the most well-intentioned leader and organization may at times veer off course. We might ignore or accept unhelpful, destructive, or unethical behavior. Make decisions that conflict with the values we should not compromise or the mission and strategic objectives of our organization. Prioritize our comfort, prestige, or self-interest over what is best for the people we lead. Silence or not listen to people who try to speak up. Bad-mouth clients or other departments. Act disingenuously or withhold critical information.

It's tempting to assume that our team members won't notice or be concerned about these inconsistencies, especially if we think they're not such a big deal, but nothing could be further from the truth.

As Alison Taylor, ethics professor at NYU Stern School of Business and author of *Higher Ground*, told me in a 2020 interview, "Employees are very attuned to hypocrisy, they're very attuned to what a leader says and how a leader behaves. So if there's a gap between stated values and what kind of behavior is actually rewarded, that will be very clear to anybody that works in the organization."[3]

Unaddressed inconsistencies fracture trust and integrity. It's often the reason why our team members roll their eyes when the company values are brought up. Even when the breach might be years in the past, it can still influence the current culture in significant ways. We mustn't simply move forward and assume that broken trust or a lack of cultural health will heal by itself. We must have the courage to address these issues directly.

The Reluctance to Confront Trust Issues

In her insightful TED Talk, Becky Kennedy, a clinical psychologist and author of the bestselling parenting guide *Good Inside*, argues that the single most important parenting strategy is to get good at repair. Since every parent will mess up and act in ways that create disconnection with their child, they must become experts at taking ownership and repairing broken trust.[4]

I've had some of the most heartfelt conversations with my eldest daughter after I've taken ownership of and apologized for ways I've failed and made mistakes as a parent—whether it's because I became too heated in a conversation, assumed things in a situation when I should have been listening, or had my priorities wrong and failed to give her the focus and attention she needed.

I'm convinced that getting great at repair is equally important in leadership. Let's explore three common scenarios I think many of us have encountered:

1. Forgetting to invite a team member to a meeting they saw as critical to their role
2. Failing to explicitly give someone credit for their contribution
3. Inadvertently signaling favoritism toward a specific team member due to a personal connection. While these

breaches of trust might seem minor, they can build up mistrust and resentment that could have been mitigated if the leader would have promptly addressed the issue and worked toward repairing trust as soon as they became aware of the breach.

However, I've found that many leaders struggle with the concept of seeking repair and apologizing. When I bring up the topic, I often hear things such as, "Why should I address this? We shouldn't focus on the negative, should we? People have already forgotten and moved on! It wasn't that big of a deal anyway. People need to get tougher skin."

Perhaps, we're afraid of how seeking repair might cast us in a negative light, or we're scared of losing control, worried about undermining our credibility and authority, or frightened of being seen as incompetent. Additionally, I think many of us want to avoid having to deal with regrets because they bring discomfort and can seem to slow us down.

Some people even claim they have no regrets. A few take it a step further and get a "no regrets" tattoo. You would be surprised to know how many regret that decision later.[5] However, while regret comes with discomfort and pain, it's an important signal that can help clarify our beliefs and values. Yes, you probably tried your best. Yes, you might have had good intentions. Yes, you have hopefully learned from the experience. But that doesn't mean you shouldn't regret the harm you inflicted, whether great or small.

Daniel H. Pink, author of the bestselling book *The Power of Regret*, drawing on research in psychology, neuroscience, economics, and biology, told me in a 2022 interview that when we start to feel regret, "we ignore it and pretend it's not a real signal, or if that doesn't work for very long, we end up wallowing in it, which is bad too. What we want to do is to confront it and face it."[6] He found that if we acknowledge and confront our regret, we can move forward with greater clarity on what should be truly important in our leadership. And when we acknowledge it and seek repair with the harmed party, our team members can move forward and trust can be restored.

Mastering the Art of Repair

A client wanted to improve their organization's ability to take risks and innovate. A culture analysis revealed an echo from the past. In several comments, we saw how the actions of one former leader's destructive leadership behavior years ago continued to affect people's ability to feel psychologically safe, take risks, and speak up.

Our team encouraged the executive team to address the past. To say that they were reluctant is an understatement. The CEO was new in his role, and many executives felt their team members should have moved on. Not surprisingly, they wanted to focus on the future and avoid bringing up negative things from the past. However, the CEO courageously decided to address the history. After we presented the result of the culture analysis in a company-wide meeting, the CEO took the stage. He mentioned the destructive leadership in the past and acknowledged the harm it had done without going into details. Then he said, "What happened was not OK nor was our silence. On behalf of our company, I want to apologize and make sure we don't ever allow that again."

I'm sure few in the executive team believed they would get much of a response. However, as soon as the CEO finished, team members rushed forward to tell their stories. Some couldn't hold back tears, grateful that the deafening silence was finally broken.

I shared this story with trust researcher Professor Sandra J. Sucher at Harvard Business School.

Sucher found that while leaders often fear apologizing because they believe it will be used against them, apologizing actually improves the perception and trust in the organization that made a mistake.[7]

However, according to Sucher, it's not enough to say, "Some mistakes were made." Instead, you must "come to terms yourself, as a leader, with the harm you've created."[8] Even when "it's not your fault, it is your problem." You must resist the urge to make up reasons why it "wasn't that bad."

For an apology to be effective, it must include these three elements:[9]

1. *Acknowledge the harm you've created, allowed, or overlooked and offer a sincere apology.* This ensures that the person on the other side can believe you understand the harm you've caused. It must be genuine and clearly express the emotions and regret you feel about the situation.
2. *Explain what went wrong.* People want to know that you understand what caused the harm; otherwise, they have no reason to trust you again. It has to be honest, straightforward, and free from defensiveness.
3. *Make an offer of repair.* This might take two forms: One is what you might potentially do for the harmed party. The other is how you will fix the process or make changes in your leadership so it won't happen again.

Let's look at two examples of apologies that include the three elements on page 91:

- "I'm so sorry I didn't invite you to the meeting. We haven't had your function in these meetings before, and I forgot that you obviously should have been included. Are you available for me to go through what we discussed?"
- "I'm very sorry for not recognizing your efforts during the client meeting. It's embarrassing to admit, but I was stressed and too focused on my own contribution and wanting to make a good impression. In our next meeting, I would like for you to take the lead and have an opportunity to talk more in detail about the work you've been doing."

As I emphasized earlier, trust is an essential form of capital for every leader. However trust is also a vulnerable relationship and can easily be broken. The good news is that it can also be restored.

To be a values-driven, trustworthy leader who cares effectively for your cultural health, you need to consistently practice and master the art of seeking repair—not only when your back is against the wall, but as soon as you realize that your actions, either through commission or omission, have been in conflict with your values, might have negatively influenced your team, and have contributed to a breach of trust.

By getting humble—embracing vulnerability and taking ownership and action to repair broken trust— we can avoid pitfalls, begin to transform our cultural health, and ensure it's sustained over the long term.

You Can Culture   Month 3

Reflection

- Reflect on a situation where you fell short of your values, treated someone unfairly, disregarded cultural challenges, or tolerated unhelpful or destructive behavior.
- What potential harm (whether minor or significant) could it have inflicted on your team or others?
- How did you react? What fears might have kept you from addressing the issue and actively working to repair broken trust?

Action

- If you've identified a situation or area in your leadership that requires attention and action to repair broken trust, I urge you to take that step.
- Commit to becoming swift and skillful at seeking repair instead of allowing issues to go unaddressed. Consider the changes and challenges you observe over time.

The Practice at a Glance

When we fail to act in line with our mission and values, overlook cultural challenges, or cause harm, we need to repair broken trust and our cultural health by (1) acknowledging the harm we've contributed to and offering a sincere apology, (2) explaining what went wrong, and (3) clarifying how we will act differently in the future. Even if the fault is not directly ours, addressing the issue is our responsibility.

" *We mustn't simply move forward and assume that broken trust or a lack of cultural health will heal by itself. We must have the courage to address these issues directly.* "

Further Resources

Books:

- *The Power of Trust: How Companies Build It, Lose It, Regain It* by Sandra J. Sucher and Shalene Gupta
- *The Power of Regret: How Looking Backward Moves Us Forward* by Daniel H. Pink

Podcasts:

- "Trust—How Companies Build It, Lose It, Regain It"—my interview with Sandra J. Sucher on the *Leading Transformational Change* podcast
- "Unlocking the Power of Regret"—my interview with Daniel H. Pink on the *Leading Transformational Change* podcast

VISIT **YOUCANCULTURE.COM**
FOR MORE RESOURCES.

HABIT 1
Get
Humble

HABIT 2
Get
Clear

CULTURAL
HEALTH

HABIT 3
Get
Listening

HABIT 4
Get
Integrity

Habit 2
Get Clear

Maturity is achieved when a person postpones immediate pleasures for long-term values.[1]

—Rabbi Joshua L. Liebman

8

The Accidental CEO, the Turnaround, and the Art of Celebration

He was an accidental CEO, he told me. When Frank Blake, then an executive vice president, received the call to take over as CEO and chairman of the Home Depot in January 2007, he was in complete surprise.[1] The Atlanta-based home improvement giant was going through severe turmoil. After a conflict with the board and deep dissatisfaction among the company's associates and shareholders, they had just ousted their previous CEO, Robert "Bob" Nardelli. They needed someone quickly, and Blake, then a fifty-eight-year-old down-to-earth, straight-shooting lawyer, was the one they chose.

"Taking care of our people" and "excellent customer service" were two of the eight values that guided the Home Depot as it began with two stores in Atlanta in 1979. Cofounders Bernie Marcus and Arthur Blank believed the most important principle to the company's success was how it cared for its associates. Arthur

Blank said in an interview, "The culture was everything that separated us from really all the competition we had."[2] He believed that the good financial result and growth they experienced (being one of the fastest-growing companies in the United States year after year) was not because they pegged their sales numbers but their values. The Home Depot offered stock options to its associates and had numerous ways of recognizing and rewarding aspiring up-and-comers. The leadership empowered their associates to do whatever it took to make the customer happy. Associates who excelled in customer service would receive colorful badges to put on their orange aprons, which donned the words "I put customers first."

There are numerous stories of how associates went to great lengths to serve their customers, such as a man who came into a Home Depot, located in a building that had once housed a tire store, asking for a refund for a set of tires.[3] There was just one problem: the Home Depot didn't sell tires. The sales associate asked his manager for advice. To his surprise, the manager told him to ask the customer how much he had paid for the tires and give him the money. The tires were later hung over the service desk as a reminder to put customers first.

in 2000, Bob Nardelli was hired as the new CEO of the Home Depot. Nardelli, who had spent thirty years at General Electric (GE), was expected to get professional management in place. GE was known to have a cutthroat culture hyperfocused on performance. As CEO, Nardelli *overfocused* on the processes and swept aside the elements of the culture that made the Home Depot special.[4] Historically, the company had a practice of employing people with experience as handymen who would go above and beyond to help their customers. Nardelli chose to cut back on these higher-paid full-time team members and replaced them with less-experienced part-time workers to lower costs and increase profits. He decreased investments in the employees, and in doing so, he also removed focus from the company's commitment to customer service. In 2005 the Home Depot plummeted to an all-time low in the American Consumer Satisfaction Index[5]—an incredible blow to a company built around customer service. The market capitalization declined radically, and the Home Depot was being outperformed by its main competitor, Lowe's. In January 2007, Nardelli was ousted by the board.

The day after being named the new CEO, Frank Blake was scheduled to record a video message for the company's 350,000 employees. He asked his son, a company store manager, for some advice. "No idea, Dad, but I'll tell you what I do in all our weekly meetings. I read something from *Built from Scratch*," his son answered. *Built from Scratch* is a book by Bernie Marcus and Arthur Blank about the story, values, and culture of the Home Depot. As Blake began to read, he found a picture of an inverted pyramid, a management philosophy that put the CEO at the bottom and the customers and sales associates at the top. Marcus would later tell Blake,

> "Remember that you have a prominent job but not a significant job. The only significant jobs are the people who are interacting with the customers."[6]

Blake instinctively knew that this was what he was supposed to talk to his team members about. He showed the picture of the inverted pyramid and spent the rest of his tenure trying to find out what it truly meant to lead from the bottom of the pyramid. He realized that gravity wasn't his friend, and he couldn't just assume that vision would cascade down through the organization. Instead, he needed to be highly intentional about discovering what mattered to the people on the front line who served the customers.

Blake spent significant time visiting and working in the stores and started meeting almost weekly with associates over lunch or dinner. He realized that the company's true purpose was wealth creation for its associates and that the most fundamental cultural assumption was that team members could trust the company to take care of them and their future. Blake told me in a 2023 interview,

> "Our associates had come to the conclusion that the company did not care much about them. There had been a series of things that had been taken away from them, in terms of compensation and recognition. So we started investing in their compensation again. We did lots of recognition and celebration programs and were very intentional about the process of thanking them for their efforts."[7]

Blake understood that reaffirming this commitment through action would be critical to getting buy-in and alignment. He realized that senior leaders often burden their team members with conflicting values and priorities. While it's easy to claim you value excellent customer service, many retail executives instead measure and celebrate a low level of theft in the stores, leading team members to focus on policing their customers. Blake realized that he needed to absorb complexity—for example, accepting a higher level of theft—to keep employees focused on serving the customer.

Blake also began a weekly ritual of writing about one hundred personal notes every Sunday afternoon to associates all over the country who had shown outstanding dedication to customer service.

This habit of writing personal notes spread to other managers at the company, creating a powerful process around celebrating people who lived the values of customer service. Blake told me he learned one of his most important leadership lessons:

"Every business understands that you get what you measure," but "what is perhaps an even more powerful principle is that you get what you celebrate."

When Blake left the Home Depot in 2014, its market capitalization had grown from $50 billion to $125 billion. In the last two years of his tenure, he was named a Top 50 CEO by Glassdoor based on reviews from employees.[8] The president of the National Retail Federation said that Blake "epitomizes the inspirational leader. He has led the Home Depot humbly, earning the respect and admiration of those privileged to work with him. The Home Depot's growth and success since he took the reins is astounding."[9]

Frank Blake's time at the Home Depot is, in my mind, a great tale of the power of getting clear on what we value through our daily leadership actions. As we explored in chapter 1, our culture is shaped by signals of what is encouraged, rewarded, tolerated, or not accepted. To build and sustain our cultural health, we must be very clear and highly intentional about those signals. And that is what we'll explore in the coming three practices.

Many values statements are vague, disconnected from the mission, and seldom prioritized or consistently adhered to, leading to a lack of integrity and clarity around cultural priorities and hindering strategy execution. To build and sustain cultural health, we must clarify our most important values, celebrate the right behaviors, and deal with unhelpful or destructive behavior.

Practices to Get Clear

In this quarter, we will explore the following three monthly practices to help transform your cultural health.

Practice 4: Make Values Matter

To make our values matter and shape our culture, we must be clear on what we are unwilling to compromise and identify behaviors crucial for delivering on our mission and strategy. This necessitates an ongoing process of reflection, leading by example even when it becomes costly, and contextualizing our values to ensure their relevance in the daily work lives of our team members.

Practice 5: Celebrate the Right Behaviors

We get what we celebrate. By actively and consistently recognizing and celebrating behaviors that align with our mission and values, we bolster employee engagement and help align our culture with our strategic objectives and most important values. It requires a creative approach, a dedicated focus on the culture we aspire to build, and a sincere investment in understanding and valuing our team members.

Practice 6: Deal with Unhelpful or Destructive Behavior

Unchecked unhelpful or destructive behavior, especially when demonstrated by high performers, tends to spread. To cultivate cultural health, we must give caring, humble, and direct feedback and be consistent and transparent in dealing with unhelpful or destructive behavior. We must pledge to only communicate values we are truly committed to adhere to even when it gets costly.

Practice 4:
Make Values Matter

When Values Become Costly

On February 23, 1943, Austrian farmer Franz Jägerstätter was called to active duty as a soldier in the Nazi Reich. He refused. On August 9, he was executed, seen as a traitor.

The movie *A Hidden Life* by director Terence Malik is a three-hour-long visually spectacular but haunting portrayal of what it meant for Franz and his family to stand up for his beliefs and values in a world entirely hostile to his convictions.[1] We see the internal struggle as Franz and his wife, Franziska, agonize over his decision to refuse service in the army. Because of that commitment, his family suffers brutal persecution from their neighbors. Even the people Jägerstätter expected to support their decision turn their backs on them out of fear. We see how people in power try to break Franz's resolve through increasingly violent measures. As the movie progresses, it becomes clear that there will be no "Hollywood moment" when the entire village sees the light and gathers to celebrate the Jägerstätter family. In the eyes of their neighbors and the leadership of their country, Franz is not a hero but a traitor. Someone who has failed his duty as a husband and a father. It would take several decades after his death before the Jägerstätter family finally received restitution.

Franz didn't become a conscientious objector because he desired martyrdom. He made the decision because he loved Austria, his country, and couldn't stomach pledging allegiance to the Nazis, who were in conflict with his deeply held beliefs and values.[2]

I've met people who sacrificed much for their values—a Ukrainian priest who, amid the Russian army bombing his town in 2022, evacuated his family but stayed behind to ensure his parishioners could get to safety before finally reuniting with his wife and three kids; a manager who bravely spoke up against the corrupt behavior of her employer, becoming a whistleblower despite losing her job and facing personal and financial devastation;[3] a professor who left a coveted professorship at Oxford because he couldn't, in good conscience, teach political integrity and ethics while holding a role paid by a financier who supported a cause that conflicted with the values that role represented.[4]

These people all made costly decisions because of principles they didn't want to compromise. While their examples may seem far removed from our daily leadership experience, I mention them to make a critical point—*values that aren't allowed to cost us something aren't worth anything at all.*

If I showed up at a meeting wearing a T-shirt stating that I'm a person of integrity and creativity, I would probably be laughed out of the room. You couldn't care less about the values I advertise. However, if you were going to be in any type of professional or personal relationship with me, you would care about what values I actually live by. You would care whether I was true to my word and honest in my interactions. Nowhere would this become more apparent than in how I act when adhering to those values would come at a personal cost.

Significance of Organizational Values

In many countries over the last few decades, it has become commonplace that organizations define three to five core values—often ambiguous characteristics the organizations want to claim without any real commitment. Few could honestly say whether they uphold the values.

Yet while the concept of values has been burdened by marketing jargon and branding practices, it is far from a modern invention. For several thousands of years, people have gathered around shared principles and beliefs that have defined parameters for behaviors, priorities, and relationships within their group. These values, principles, and behaviors have been critical in their mission, growth, and cohesiveness.

So is there a suitable place and a need for values that govern organizational decisions, priorities, and behaviors? Yes, definitely, whether you call them values, principles, cultural priorities, or something else!

Because ultimately, every human and, subsequently, every culture and organization is values-driven. The question is, what values are in the driving seat?

Every leader and organization will promote some behaviors and not accept others. Every leader and organization will be drawn toward pursuing what it fundamentally sees as precious, like

Gollum to the ring in J. R. R. Tolkien's epic fantasy tale. Getting clear on what those are and reflecting on what they mean can help us be much more intentional about what our organization becomes.

A few years ago, I was invited to speak to a management team at an innovative tech scale-up undergoing an initial public offering, or IPO. Having listened to my talk on values, the CEO said he didn't like the idea of values being costly. I countered that we shouldn't define values because we believe they are inherently bad for business. However, we should get clear on values and behaviors that will help us build cultural health that enables mission success, a thriving workplace, and responsible impact—values that clarify what we believe will lead to a flourishing organization and won't compromise in our pursuit of success.

This forces us not only to focus on what's good or attractive in the short term but also to consider the long-term impact of our decisions.

We've all seen the negative impact when profit maximization, cost minimization, or selfish ambition become the defining values of an organization, and the outcomes are not pleasing.

Take the example of how Boeing, the airplane manufacturer, created a cultural pressure on cost and speed and cut corners on safety on their new 737 MAX, costing hundreds of people their lives in tragically avoidable crashes.[5] We've seen countless organizations lose momentum, face crises, and fail in their mission and strategy because they didn't consistently abide by good values.

However, we've also seen the positive power of organizations making decisions based on sound principles. We've seen companies that have staked out impressive market positions, become highly attractive employers, and proved themselves very resilient, at least partly, because they—as in the example of Frank Blake and the Home Depot—made their values matter.

While organizational values are important, we should not attempt to police people's thoughts or opinions in conflict with fundamental principles such as the freedoms of opinion, expression, or religion. However, we need to be clear on how we should operate and work together and what behaviors lead to success. Louise Bringselius, an author on culture and values and acclaimed trust researcher at Lund University, told me, "Every individual has the right to her values, but not to her behavior in an organizational context."[6]

Having helped many organizations get clear on values and behaviors, our team has learned that for organizational values/principles to be valuable, they should:

1. clarify what is most important, not just what seems most urgent;
2. be principles we're not willing to sacrifice, even when costly;
3. remain true to who we are as an organization;
4. align with our mission and strategy;
5. be lived with integrity by the leadership;
6. guide what behaviors we should encourage or not tolerate; and
7. encourage hard conversations about trade-offs and dilemmas.

Hopefully, your organization's values align with every item on that list. Regardless of whether they do, remember that it's not the language but the application that matters most. As leaders, we have a responsibility to ensure that sound values drive our leadership, team, and organization.

Four Different but Essential Types of Values

I asked several executive teams to brainstorm a list of values they would want politicians to lead by, regardless of their political persuasion. The lists were rather similar. They wanted leaders who are honest, humble, and willing to admit that they're wrong (that's a big ask, I know); who seek what's in the best interest of the nation and not themselves; who have the courage to make needed long-term investments; who take responsibility and avoid blaming others for their failures; and who are respectful and create a psychologically safe environment for their teams to thrive and get the best ideas on the table. I'm sure you would agree that the above things are desirable not just for politicians but for anyone in leadership.

While organizational values may differ based on strategic differences (for example, values in excellent customer service might be immensely important in a retail business but not the most important value in a government regulatory agency), there are fundamental values that people across geographies and cultures see as desirable and important. The late professor and ethicist Rushworth Kidder, author of *Moral Courage*, conducted extensive research on cross-cultural values and summarized the most commonly shared ones into five: *honesty, respect, responsibility, fairness,* and *compassion.*[7]

While we may disagree on the implications and applications of these values, I think most of us would agree that our team members want these values to be integral to their teams and organizations. Many would also resonate deeply with other values, for example virtues within several faith traditions, such as courage, humility, justice, and self-restraint.

On top of that, different types of sectors and professions may have specific values and ethical codes as well.

Moreover, we, as leaders, and our team members have individual values that shape us. Research shows an increased risk of burnout when there's a discrepancy between personal and organizational values.[8]

I mention this to argue that leading and making decisions based on values is not as simple as just relating to our organizational values.

For us to be values-driven leaders, we need to be cognizant of the following:

1. The fundamental values that are universally important
2. The individual values that are personally important
3. The organizational values that are strategically important
4. The role or industry-related values that are important to our specific sector or profession

---

There will be times when these values may come into conflict. During those times, knowing what we won't compromise, even when other values are at stake, becomes incredibly important. We can't allow ourselves to entertain the excuse, "It's not personal . . . it's strictly business" (as the famous line from the movie *The Godfather* goes).

Our decisions and behaviors at work are personal.
They influence who we are and who we become.
If we continually compromise important values,
we will become increasingly desensitized,
which will impact our moral compass.

Making Values-Driven Decisions

As leaders, we face situations where our values get tested. We face a talent shortage and are considering hiring someone who might not represent the values our organization claims. While we know a specific solution would serve the client better, our profitability is much higher on a different service. We experience dysfunction or elements of toxic behaviors in our team, but we would prefer not to deal with it.

Carolyn Taylor, a pioneer in organizational culture and the author of *Walking the Talk*, told me in a 2020 interview that a person or organization that is values-driven:

> "lives by a set of principles that are strong enough to cause them to make sacrifices in order to uphold them. Somebody who is not values-driven will ultimately put their own survival first, whatever that survival means—remaining popular, continuing to make money, getting ahead in business, winning, or something else that is self-serving. They will compromise and take expedient action in order to achieve a certain outcome."[9]

Being a values-driven leader doesn't mean we always get it right, but we humbly and courageously wrestle with integrating our values into decisions, such as the following:

- Should we spend resources on this initiative?
- Should we recruit this person?
- Should we sell to this client?
- Should we buy from this supplier?
- Should we go into this partnership?
- Should we tolerate this behavior?
- Should we celebrate and incentivize this behavior?

However, many decisions are in the gray zone, and there may be many different stakeholder perspectives to consider.

One organization that is known for being intentionally values-driven (not to say they do it perfectly) is IKEA, the €44.6 billion (2021) Swedish home-furnishing giant. They've built much of their historical success around values such as cost consciousness, simplicity, and caring for people and planet—values that relate intimately to their vision: "To create a better everyday life for the many people."

I had a conversation with Giovanni Leoni, the global head of algorithm and AI ethics at Inter IKEA Group. His team's responsibility is to support the organization in making values-driven decisions in their use of artificial intelligence. Since AI is a quickly developing field, much of the work is in ambiguity and the gray zone. So how do you make your values matter in such a fast-changing environment?

Instead of putting themselves as judges of the ethicality of all use of AI across the company, Leoni explained that the team seeks to empower the whole company to make values-driven decisions. At the core is a simple values-driven leadership framework with three sequential steps, using the symbolism of the gut, the mind, and the heart. The gut signifies the need to develop a gut reaction when encountering a situation when using AI could entail values dilemmas and ethical concerns, prompting individuals to pause and reflect. They establish this gut reaction by consistently making team members reflect on how they apply their values in their personal use of technology. The mind signifies researching and getting needed competence from digital ethics expertise and other functions. The heart symbolizes IKEA's culture and values, serving as a guide, even when there is no clear-cut answer, to help ask the right questions and ultimately make the best possible decisions toward a good end.

I believe this simple framework can be equally helpful in other organizations.

Six Questions for Better Decisions

As discussed in chapter 2, numerous factors can impede our capacity to make values-driven decisions, even with good intentions (ethical fading, group pressure, moral licensing, etc.). To enhance our ability to make decisions aligned with our values and engage our gut, mind, and heart, it is helpful to ask ourselves specific questions as we reflect on our decisions.

Here are six questions that I think can be particularly useful:

1. What would a great leader do in this situation?
2. Does this decision align with my/our values?
3. Who is potentially impacted by my decision, and have they been consulted?

4. What might be the negative or unintended consequences of this decision?
5. How would I feel about this decision if it were to become public knowledge?
6. How will I feel about this decision five years from now?

Personally, reflecting on what a great leader would do in a specific decision helps me take an outside perspective and connect with the leader I aspire to be. The president of a nonprofit told me that he and his team members regularly do the *New York Times* test, considering how the decision would be portrayed if it ended up on the cover of a major newspaper.

While we need to recognize that making values-aligned decisions is challenging and a constant wrestle, asking ourselves similar questions helps us to intentionally and constructively engage in that struggle. And by doing so, we train ourselves to make better decisions.

Four Ways to Make Values Matter

Making values matter involves more than just listing attributes such as integrity and innovation. It entails engaging in an ongoing conversation about what should be important to both ourselves, our team, and our organization and what changes are necessary to live according to those principles. Here are four things we can all do to make our values matter:

1 **Get clear on what the values are.**

Make sure you have a clear understanding of the different types of values mentioned earlier. Reflect on your personal values. Engage with literature, art, movies, or podcasts that can help you reflect on life's big questions, moral dilemmas, and what kind of leader and person you aspire to be.

Familiarize yourself with your organization's values and codes of conduct. Make it a weekly practice to read through and reflect on them. If any aspects seem unclear, ask questions to initiate conversations with your colleagues or superiors about what these values mean to your organization and your team members.

2 **Lead by example.**

It's evident that organizational values will only matter if we lead by example. However, too often, companies market their values to change employee behavior without addressing the misalignment between leadership's words and actions. I discussed this with Maria Hemberg, a member of the executive management team at Volvo Cars, the Swedish car manufacturer known for being a world leader in safety, who managed to make it an integral value at the company. An essential part of that, Hemberg told me, is to get people to lead by example. She compared it to parenting, noting that if you tell your children to eat candy only on Saturdays, but you eat candy on Wednesdays, they'll follow your example and not your words.[10] Guilty as charged. Leading by example necessitates:

1. continuously reflecting on how organizational values should influence behavior and decisions;

2. acknowledging our own struggles and blind spots related to our values;
3. committing to being consistent in thoughts, words, and actions; and
4. taking ownership when we fail.

3 **Contextualize the values.**

Values become clear in our behaviors. Melissa Daimler, chief learning officer at Udemy and author of *ReCulturing*, has spent a significant part of her career helping fast-growing tech companies such as Twitter and Adobe get clear on and align their organizations with their strategic values-driven behaviors. She told me in a 2023 interview,

> "When we clarify values-based behaviors, everyone within our organization can understand how they are supposed to work and interact to succeed in our environment."[11]

However, we must ensure that these behaviors are observable, allowing us to see people actively acting on them, and applicable, so people know what they mean. For instance, what does it mean to act in line with these values and behaviors when someone is negotiating with a supplier, working on the production line, writing code, treating a patient, or having a sales meeting with a client? If we can't make the values and behaviors meaningful in these situations, they won't have any significance. To contextualize our values, I suggest selecting a specific behavior, such as "engaging in constructive disagreements," and reflecting on how you can make it clear to your team. Consider what support they might need to act in line with this behavior. Then move on to the next. If you don't have those behaviors clearly defined, then you need to start by making them explicit.

4 Ask questions to reflect on your decisions.

As I've stated before, we can't just assume we make values-driven decisions. Using questions such as, "Who is potentially impacted by my decision, and have they been consulted?" will help us make better and more values-driven decisions.

I would like to conclude by repeating something mentioned at the beginning of this practice. Values that aren't allowed to cost us something aren't worth anything at all. It is through our intentional and consistent engagement with the principles and behaviors we refuse to compromise that our values become valuable.

You Can Culture   Month 4

Reflection

- Personal values: What personal core values guide your decision-making and actions as a leader?
- Organizational values: What steps would you need to take to empower your team members to better apply the organizational values in their specific contexts?
- Decision-making: What strategies could you employ to help ensure you deliberately make values-driven decisions even under pressure?

Action

- Commit to one consistent action to make values matter more in your leadership and for your team members. Consider the changes and challenges you observe over time.

The Practice at a Glance

To make our values matter and shape our culture, we must be clear on what we are unwilling to compromise and identify behaviors crucial for delivering on our mission and strategy. This necessitates an ongoing process of reflection, leading by example even when it becomes costly, and contextualizing our values to ensure their relevance in the daily work lives of our team members.

" *Values that aren't allowed to cost us something aren't worth anything at all.* "

Further Resources

Books:

- *Walking the Talk: Building a Culture for Success* by Carolyn Taylor
- *ReCulturing: Design Your Company Culture to Connect with Strategy and Purpose for Lasting Success* by Melissa Daimler

Podcasts:

- "The Values-Driven Leader"—my interview with Carolyn Taylor on the *Leading Transformational Change* podcast
- "The IKEA Values, AI, and Operating in the Unknown"—my interview with Giovanni Leoni on the *Leading Transformational Change* podcast
- "Design Your Company Culture to Connect with Values, Strategy, and Purpose"—my interview with Melissa Daimler on the *Leading Transformational Change* podcast
- "Leading with Values at Volvo Cars"—my interview with Maria Hemberg on the *Leading Transformational Change* podcast

VISIT **YOUCANCULTURE.COM**
FOR MORE RESOURCES.

10

Practice 5: Celebrate the Right Behaviors

"Let me tell you about the proudest moment in my career at this company. We had been trying to improve at change and innovation, but we are entrenched in how things have always been done around here. My team had, on their own initiative, made adjustments to create a little more effective flow in their production area. It wasn't anything major but a big deal to them. I told my boss about their efforts, and he suggested that we go to take a look at the changes. My team was beaming with pride as they told us about what they were trying to accomplish and what they had learned. Seeing my team's excitement that day was the proudest moment of my career."

This inspiring story was shared by a line manager during our interview about the culture at her manufacturing company. It shows the power of recognizing and celebrating desired behavior, emphasizing that such acknowledgment can be as simple yet powerful as a manager showing a genuine interest in someone's work and curiously asking them about it.

When we help organizations assess their cultural health, we often ask team members what behaviors and initiatives they perceive as encouraged and incentivized within their organization. On several occasions, we're excited to see clear patterns of positive behavior that a large percentage of team members agree are encouraged. Oftentimes, this correlates with these behaviors being strong cultural traits at the organization—for example, serving the customer with excellence, delivering a high-quality product, or collaborating across departments and geographies.

However, too often, a significant percentage of team members say they don't see any specific behaviors being encouraged and celebrated. When we present these findings to the executive team, they often realize that, despite wanting to assume they do an excellent job of employee recognition, they've never had a strategic conversation about which behaviors should be encouraged or how they can be intentional and creative about it. They've presumed that every manager should have this knowledge instinctively.

Yet a 2013, Glassdoor study of two thousand adults revealed that 53 percent of employees would stay longer at their company if they felt more appreciation from their manager, and 81 percent of employees stated they were motivated to work harder when their boss expressed appreciation for their work.[1]

As we will see throughout this practice, recognizing positive behaviors doesn't have to be complicated or expensive. However, it can have immensely positive effects on our ability to fulfill our mission, bolster employee engagement, and build a thriving workplace.

A Culture of Intentional Celebration

It was a dreadful day. A sales meeting in Stockholm didn't go as anticipated, and now I needed to hurry to the train station for a four-and-a-half-hour journey back to our home in the southern city of Malmö, Sweden. I hopped on an electric rental scooter, securing my new iPhone in a holder to rely on Google Maps for directions. Unfortunately, the phone holder malfunctioned, causing my precious device to slip right in the middle of an intersection—only to be run over by a passing bus. (What are the odds, right?) Upon reaching the train station, I discovered my train was delayed and opted to wait in a coffee shop, hoping to catch up on work while keeping an eye on the departure times. Just when I thought things couldn't get worse, the train mysteriously vanished from the digital board. Sprinting to the platform, I realized the train had left, leaving me and a crowd of disgruntled passengers stranded. With no other options (since my wife was leaving for Paris the next morning and I couldn't leave our two youngest kids home alone), I reluctantly paid a small fortune for a last-minute flight back home.

Arriving very late at night, I was frustrated with myself and disappointed about my day. However, instead of facing criticism or snarky remarks, I was met with encouragement and even celebration by my wife and eldest daughter. They reminded me why I had gone on that trip, how I earnestly had tried to address the challenges of the potential client, and that the iPhone was a replaceable object.

While I tend to be overly self-critical, focusing on my mistakes, my wife believes strongly in encouraging and celebrating.

It's not about avoiding hard conversations or overlooking bad behavior; rather, it's about cultivating an environment where recognizing positive behaviors is the default, creating a space where it's safe to make mistakes and embrace vulnerability.

This culture of celebration has literally changed my life. Having grown up in a destructive community with an increasingly toxic culture, I was used to an environment where almost every failure or mistake I made was scrutinized and criticized. I have been in countless meetings where perceived issues or flaws, whether mine or someone else's, were dissected by the founder in front of a large group for hours. Questioning anything was met with turning my mistakes against me to silence me. I'm sure you understand what this can do to a person's mind and heart. It instills fear and wrecks confidence. You start hiding your mistakes and silencing yourself.

Fortunately, most of you have not encountered such a toxic workplace environment. Undoubtedly, you realize the immense value of recognizing and encouraging your team members.

Yet, I implore all of us to be even more deliberate in celebrating the right behaviors, as it holds the potential for profound positive impact on our cultural health.

Reflect on Stan Slap's definition of culture that I shared in chapter 1: "Culture is a living organism that constantly gathers information to confirm its perception of reality, ensure its survival and emotional well-being." This implies that your team members are constantly seeking signals to guide them toward success and help them understand what it takes to feel included in your team and organization. These signals have an immense impact on shaping your culture. And yet, we're often not intentional enough about the signals we send.

A study by Gallup and Workhuman found that while employee recognition is a fundamental employee need, "only one in four worldwide strongly agree they have received recognition for their work in the last week. When organizations move that bar up to six in ten, they stand to gain a 28 percent improvement in quality and 31 percent reduction in absenteeism."[2] They found that most employees wanted to be recognized at least a few times a month; however, this is not the benchmark but a "bare minimum."

> *Their data showed that "there's no such thing as too much recognition—as long as it's genuine and appropriately given."*

I'm not suggesting that you shy away from holding people accountable or distribute participation trophies to team members who don't deliver. What I am advocating, however, is that you commit to mastering the art of catching people doing the right thing and recognizing them for it. I've met experienced senior executives who desperately wanted to get some form of feedback and acknowledgment from their boss, seeking assurance that their work was valued. However, asking a superior for more positive feedback can feel uncomfortable and outright scary, to say the least.

While celebrating and providing positive feedback might not be second nature to you, I'm confident that, like me, you can learn and grow. And when we do, our team, culture, and the mission and performance of our organization stand to gain significantly.

Celebration as a Tool for Culture Change

When you see a need for change in your culture, it's tempting to list a hundred different behaviors and actions and then get to work on trying to change or implement all of them. However, this approach is prone to failure due to a lack of focus.

The late Professor Emeritus Edgar Schein told me, in a 2021 interview, that the way companies approach culture change, aiming to radically transform their entire culture, is akin to someone asking you to change your whole personality. While that is an outrageous ask, we do, however, have the power to change a specific behavior, and this can become a catalyst for achieving much more significant change.[3]

I often encourage leaders to concentrate on one to three specific positive behaviors to begin or do more of to evolve the culture in the right direction over six to twelve months. This idea aligns with research on keystone habits, made famous by Charles Duhigg's bestselling book *The Power of Habit*. Duhigg explains that

> "Keystone habits start a process that, over time, transforms everything. Keystone habits say that success doesn't depend on getting every single thing right, but instead relies on identifying a few key priorities and fashioning them into powerful levers."[4]

For example, establishing the habit of exercising regularly often also helps you have better dietary habits and sleep patterns. Jon Katzenbach writes in *The Critical Few* that keystone behaviors in an organizational context are "a few carefully identified things that some people do, day after day, that would lead your company to succeed if they were replicated at greater scale."[5] This was precisely the strategy that Frank Blake instinctively used as he created a process for celebrating extraordinary customer service at the Home Depot.

Let's consider an example. An orthopedics company was grappling with issues related to us-versus-them behavior. Upon assessing their culture, they realized that clinic workers helping fit patients with orthopedic braces and support receive praise and sometimes even physical gifts from grateful patients. While this was something to be proud of, many others in the organization felt disconnected from the patients and struggled to see how their work mattered. The clinic workers would also use their close relationship with the patients as an excuse for bad-mouthing others within the company. The leadership identified a positive behavior that could help break this pattern—letting clinic workers share the praise and gratitude received with the whole organization, allowing everyone to see how their work contributed to satisfied clients and company success. A simple behavior that, if turned into a habit, would drive powerful change.

Once we have defined the critical behaviors, we need to be intentional and consistent in encouraging and celebrating them until they become habits central to our culture. This ensures that everyone is aware of what cultural change we are striving for, understands how they can contribute, and knows that their contribution will be recognized.

When Celebrating the Right Behavior Becomes a Defining Moment

When the executive team at Airbnb, a global home-rental giant, observed the scandals plaguing other successful Silicon Valley start-ups, such as Uber, they realized that their company was not immune to the same problems. So they decided to emphasize integrity as a fundamental part of the Airbnb culture.

General Counsel and Chief Ethics Officer Rob Chesnut named the initiative Integrity Belongs Here, coupling it with the mission of "belonging" that was fundamental to the company. He realized that every organization has what he calls "integrity moments," where values get tested in a way that could significantly impact the culture. The moments when the company gets it right need to be recognized and celebrated.

Chesnut bought beautiful YETI water bottles with the slogan "Integrity Belongs Here" to give as gifts to team members who asked good ethics-related questions or raised ethical concerns. An illustrative example involves a day when Chesnut, working at his desk at the Airbnb headquarters, briefly stepped away for a bathroom break, leaving his computer open and unlocked. Returning to his table, he was informed by a midlevel IT manager, in a friendly way, that not locking his computer was a security violation. At first Chesnut wanted to get defensive and fire back, but he stopped himself and realized how much courage it took for this manager to call out an executive team member for a security violation.

In the next company meeting, Chesnut told everyone his violation story and how he was grateful that the IT manager had the courage to call him out on it. He asked the man to stand up, awarded him a YETI water bottle, and applauded with everyone. Two years later, the IT manager wrote Chesnut a note, telling him that receiving the water bottle was the proudest moment in his six years of working at the company. Chesnut told me, in a 2020 interview, that the significant thing was not the bottle itself, which cost only thirty dollars, but the message that speaking up with integrity, even if it involved misbehavior from an executive, would be celebrated.[6]

*When people realize that our values and behaviors
are more than mere words—and that their actions
will be acknowledged and celebrated—they will keep
doing those behaviors, and do them more often,
because the behavior we celebrate will multiply.*

Five Keys to Celebrating the Right Behaviors

Here are five keys to recognizing and celebrating positive
behaviors well:

1 **Understand what makes people tick.**
While bonuses, salary increases, and other financial incentives
can be powerful motivators, they are far from everything and
may not always be the most powerful recognition methods.
For example, research on self-determination theory shows
that additional factors such as getting to develop your competence and achieve mastery, increasing autonomy, and having
a sense of relatedness and purpose also contribute greatly to
employee motivation.[7]

For one person, getting more independence in planning
their work might be a powerful motivator. For another,
getting to develop and master a new skill might be even more
critical. For yet another person, getting to work on a project
that gives them a greater sense of purpose makes them feel
valued. Considering that people receive and respond to recognition differently, we need to be intentional and creative
about how we give it.

2 **Give genuine, timely, and specific positive feedback.**
Receiving positive feedback that is disingenuous or a tick-the-box exercise doesn't add any value; on the contrary, it devalues both the giver and the receiver. A great way to ensure that your feedback is genuine is by being personal, being specific about the behavior and the positive impact it had, and giving the feedback as early as possible.

Here are some examples:

- "I was greatly impressed by how you handled the client presentation. It was evident that the client was positively surprised by your thorough preparations and clear explanations."
- "Thank you for your tremendous effort in leading this project. Without your clear guidance and the way you ensured that all team members were on top of their tasks, we would never have been able to meet our deadline."
- "Thanks for the excellent collaboration. Your helpfulness, willingness to cooperate, and positive attitude toward your colleagues play a significant role in our team's success."

---

3 **Be creative about how you celebrate behavior.**
While providing specific, timely, and genuine positive feedback is probably the most common way to encourage positive behaviors, there are many other ways to celebrate them. Here are some examples:

- Highlight an initiative or an idea from a team/team member at a company meeting.
- Ask how you can support a team/team member doing good work.
- Encourage a team/team member to share what they have been learning.
- Write an encouraging note or letter.
- Give flexibility to a team/team member to focus on a specific initiative.
- Create an award that you can hand out to teams/team members showing desired behaviors.
- Take a team/team member to lunch or give them a gift card to a restaurant they appreciate.
- Give kudos or feedback on internal or external digital platforms.

4   **Focus on the direction and not the starting point.**

To encourage change, you need to be intentional about how you acknowledge progress. For a client navigating a challenging culture change, we developed a recognition strategy around the idea that what mattered most was not one's current level of perfection but whether they took a step in the right direction. This created a powerful narrative—that everyone, including the organization's senior executives, had a step to take and a reason to move.

5   **Be aware of pitfalls.**

While encouraging desired behavior is essential and powerful, you must consider unintended consequences. Here are a few pitfalls to pay attention to:

- Does the way we celebrate communicate an emphasis solely on individual performance, neglecting the importance of teamwork?
- Does the way we celebrate suggest that only novel initiatives matter and not core functions?
- Do we celebrate people who solve problems and not people who are careful about trying to mitigate problems, leading to a firefighting culture?
- Are only a few people continuously getting noticed, and are some people's behaviors left unnoticed and unrecognized because of bias or discrimination?

Ultimately, every team member, whether they would admit it, desires to be recognized for their contributions.

As a leader, you have a powerful opportunity to shape culture by intentionally celebrating the right behaviors in a genuine, timely, and specific way!

You Can Culture   Month 5

Reflection

- What behaviors should you become better at recognizing and celebrating?
- How could you do it more intentionally and creatively to strengthen team engagement and help shape your desired culture?

Action

- Commit to more intentionally recognizing and celebrating one or a few positive behaviors aligned with your mission and values. Work on improving consistency and quality and reflect on the challenges and changes you see.

The Practice at a Glance

We get what we celebrate. By actively and consistently recognizing and celebrating behaviors that align with our mission and values, we bolster employee engagement and help align our culture with our strategic objectives and most important values. It requires a creative approach, a dedicated focus on the culture we aspire to build, and a sincere investment in understanding and valuing our team members.

" *When people realize that our values and behaviors are more than mere words— and that their actions will be acknowledged and celebrated—they will keep doing those behaviors, and do them more often, because the behavior we celebrate will multiply.* "

Further Resources

Books:

- *The Critical Few: Energize Your Company's Culture by Choosing What Really Matters* by Jon Katzenbach
- *Intentional Integrity: How Smart Companies Can Lead an Ethical Revolution* by Robert Chesnut
- *Drive: The Surprising Truth About What Motivates Us* by Daniel H. Pink

Podcasts:

- "Culture Lessons from a Fortune 50 CEO"—my interview with Frank Blake on the *Leading Transformational Change* podcast
- "Intentional Integrity"—my interview with Robert Chesnut on the *Leading Transformational Change* podcast

VISIT **YOUCANCULTURE.COM**
FOR MORE RESOURCES.

11

Practice 6:
Deal with Unhelpful or Destructive Behavior

I n 2009 shocking news emerged that Johan af Donner, a communication director at the Red Cross in Sweden, embezzled about $1 million from the global nonprofit to finance a lavish lifestyle. The fact that Donner stole donated funds led to a media uproar and severe damage to the reputation of the Red Cross, with lingering consequences over a decade later. It didn't help when the media uncovered Donner's history of deceit, embezzlement, and dubious financial practices at previous employers, which the Red Cross had been aware of before recruiting him. Despite the glaring red flags, Donner's charisma and exceptional fundraising abilities, which tripled donations for the Red Cross, led people to overlook his questionable actions.[1]

When Sirkka Gustafsson, one of Donner's secretaries, found irregularities in Donner's financial dealings, she raised her concerns with the vice general secretary. However, she hesitated to escalate the issue further because she knew both the general secretary and the chairman were Donner's friends and would have his back. The Swedish Red Cross later acknowledged a prevailing culture where team members were reluctant to challenge leaders, even in the face of highly questionable expense reports.[2]

While embezzlement of nonprofit funds is, hopefully, not prevalent, overlooking misconduct from high performers is. Here are just a few of the many examples we've encountered in our work:

- A charismatic leader who outperforms his key performance indicators, or KPIs, and draws significant acclaim, but behind the scenes, he misuses his power and engages in unethical behavior
- A team of engineers responsible for the company's most important products who display a dismissive attitude toward their colleagues, hindering collaboration
- A group of longtime, loyal employees who have stopped performing efficiently and instead deliberately pass on their work to new employees
- An accomplished doctor who continually disparages nurses, even in the presence of patients
- A group of high-earning salespeople who resort to questionable business practices to secure bonuses

In almost all these examples, (1) there have been clear red flags that leaders chose to overlook; (2) the behavior has negatively affected and, in some cases, had a toxic influence on parts of the culture; (3) there has been a reluctance to deal with the behavior because of fear of confronting or disgruntling a high performer; and (4) the people in power have rationalized inaction, downplaying the effect the behavior has had on their people and their culture.

Yet research has shown that toxic cultures cost US companies almost $50 billion per year,[3] and it was the biggest driver of attrition according to the world's largest study of corporate culture by researchers at MIT.[4] Charlie Sull, cofounder of CultureX and a researcher in charge of the study, told me in a 2023 interview that "even in very healthy cultures with relatively little toxicity, addressing pockets of toxicity is often one of the highest impact ways to improve the employee experience and stop attrition. Toxicity is such a powerful driver of employee experience that even small amounts can have a significant negative impact on the culture."[5] A study by Dylan Minor at Harvard Business School showed that "avoiding a toxic employee can save a company more than twice as much as bringing on a star performer."[6]

> *While the cost of dealing with unhelpful or destructive behavior might seem substantial, the cost of inaction is often considerably higher.*

Unfortunately, we typically only see the repercussions further down the road, when our organization has already paid too high of a price.

Disregarded Bad Behaviors Will Spread

It was the confession the world of sports and millions of fans had been waiting for. Lance Armstrong, who for seven consecutive years won the Tour De France, the most famous competition in the cycling world, admitted in a tense interview with Oprah Winfrey that he had been using illegal performance-enhancing drugs. Armstrong, who became a household name worldwide after beating cancer and returning to cycling in 1998, had vehemently denied the allegations for years. He bullied and attacked anyone accusing him, calling a former support team member who had blown the whistle "an alcoholic whore."[7] While Armstrong admitted that he was doped, he claimed he didn't technically believe it was cheating because, in his mind, everyone was doing it. When asked in a BBC interview whether he would do it again, Armstrong answered, "If you would take me back to 1995 when it was completely and totally pervasive, I'd probably do it again."[8]

> *While it's true that what we celebrate will multiply, as we learned in Practice 5, it's also true that the bad behavior we disregard has an uncanny ability to spread.*

We want heroes like Armstrong, who can seemingly do the impossible and achieve the highest level, and we tend to avoid considering the dark side or taking allegations seriously. What we accept creates an environment where people can claim, "It's just the way things are done around here," about unhelpful, destructive, or even unethical behavior, whether that means someone not doing their job or engaging in harassment toward a fellow team member.

When we disregard bad behavior from people seen as having positional or informal power or being high performers, it also communicates that we don't treat people equally. Several studies have found that "toxic rock stars" can have outsize effects on minorities, and it can hamper diversity and inclusion.[9] An interviewee for a 2021 study of women of color said, "Our leaders coddle the toxic rock stars and leave the rest of us to suffer the consequences."[10] In a fascinating study on how narcissistic leadership poisons organizational culture, Professor Jennifer Chatman and colleagues found that narcissistic leaders led to "dramatically lower levels of collaboration and integrity at all levels,"[11] and perhaps more surprisingly, the effect stays even after the leader is gone.

One of the most disheartening examples of unaddressed toxic behavior in my professional experience involved an informal leader at a company who wielded his power to bully colleagues and engage in sexual harassment, a situation known to the rest of the team. Shockingly, the CEO not only turned a blind eye to these actions but also shielded the individual from consequences. In desperation, colleagues bravely reported the toxic culture to the board, only to be met with silence and inaction. The events reinforced the team's belief that speaking up didn't matter, fostering a collective trauma and perpetuating a culture of entrenched silence that proved hard to break.

Condoning Problematic Behaviors Shatters Integrity

Our tendency to overlook unhelpful or destructive behaviors often leads to the breakdown of our values and integrity.

When team members see leaders accept behavior that conflicts with organizational values, it conveys the message that the values are meaningless and undermines any effort to improve the culture.

On multiple occasions, our team has been asked to assist an organization (i.e., improve collaboration and cohesion), only to discover that one or a group of prominent leaders, high performers, or long-term employees consistently acts in direct conflict with the desired change and stonewalls any critique of their behavior. And sadly, the CEO ignores the behavior and is unwilling to challenge them. One can only imagine the frustration the situation creates with the rest of the organization, who witness the hypocrisy daily.

Several years ago, I had a project manager at a communications agency who played a vital role in our team and was genuinely committed to our mission for a number of years. However, he gradually became disengaged, redirecting his focus toward another business venture. Despite my unsuccessful attempts to prompt a change in his behavior, I hesitated to suggest that it might be better for him to part ways with the company. When I eventually mustered the courage to broach the subject, to my surprise, he was relieved, and we agreed on terms for his departure. However, it was only after he left that I recognized the negative impact my failure to address the situation had on the team and how frustrated they were that I had accepted it for so long.

I've had numerous conversations with leaders who noticed unhelpful or destructive behavior but tried to rationalize it out of fear of discomfort, reprisals, or loss of productivity. However, they were ultimately forced to act anyway because the situation became too untenable. In hindsight, they expressed regret for not addressing the issue sooner, recognizing the adverse impact it had on their organizational culture.

Six Keys to Dealing with Unhelpful Behavior

Confronting someone's behavior can be uncomfortable, so leaders often avoid it. Ideally, when the behavior is unhelpful but not entrenched (which is true in most cases), it can be sufficient to clarify its negative impact, offering individuals an opportunity for development and growth. I, for one, know I need that. Organizational psychologist Adam Grant wrote,

> *"Withholding feedback is choosing comfort over growth. Staying silent deprives people of the opportunity to learn."*[12]

We also need to be mindful of whether a team member is facing personal challenges, negatively impacting their attitude, behavior, or performance, and is in need of space and our support.

Here are six things to consider when dealing with unhelpful behavior that will help your team members learn and grow and will ensure the integrity of your culture and values.

1 Build trust and show care.

In her bestselling book *Radical Candor*, Kim Scott suggests that to help our team members grow and experience profound change, we need to care personally and be willing to provide direct feedback. However, it has to happen in that order. Otherwise, we are in danger of ending up in what she refers to as "obnoxious aggression."[13]

In Practice 7, I will make the case that we want to solicit feedback and help create a culture where we intentionally and continually invite input from our team, peers, and leaders so that we can learn and grow. By proactively seeking feedback, we demonstrate a genuine interest in others' perspectives and acknowledge our own areas for improvement. Coupled with the practice of offering authentic, timely, and specific positive feedback, as discussed in Practice 5, we not only build trust but also show that we care for our team members and their contributions.

2   Ask for permission.

To lay the groundwork for the feedback to be as helpful and effective as possible, it's advisable to ask the person for permission before you offer it.

3   Be humble and helpful.

The person who's receiving feedback will quickly feel whether your intention is to help them grow or to simply get something off your chest. Always strive to be helpful. It's equally important to be humble about the fact that you might not understand the situation perfectly or have the complete truth. I've often discovered that there are more sides to the story than I initially perceived and that I might have exhibited similar behavior that I'm now criticizing. Thus, it's crucial to begin by taking ownership of my own role, as emphasized in Practice 2.

4   Praise and solicit feedback in public and correct in private.

While it's not a perfect rule, praising and soliciting feedback in public can often be beneficial both for the person and for the overall culture. However, offering challenging feedback in public almost never is. In nearly every case, delivering critical feedback should be done privately, fostering a safe and confidential environment. As I highlighted in Practice 5, I've experienced the detrimental effects of a culture where people were consistently criticized in public.

Nevertheless, there are some situations in which publicly addressing bad behavior as it happens is needed to send a clear message to your team that this kind of behavior is unacceptable. This should, however, be done with great care. For instance, a CEO, upon overhearing an offensive joke in the lunchroom, didn't want to remain silent but also sought to avoid putting someone on the spot. Instead she decided to ask the group, "Can you help me understand what was so funny?" Using questions such as "Is this in line with our values?" or "Is this the kind of organization we want to be?" can be helpful to respectfully address behavior in a public setting.

5 Situation-Behavior-Impact

When you've shown that you care, that you desire to be humble and helpful, and that you've created the right environment, you might see the need to give some constructive or corrective feedback. While there are many helpful feedback frameworks, I've chosen to recommend the research-backed Situation-Behavior-Impact (SBI) model developed by the Center for Creative Leadership because it's straightforward, easy to remember, and "is proven to reduce the anxiety of delivering feedback and also reduce the defensiveness of the recipient."[14]

1. **Situation**
   Describe the specific situation and include the time and place in which the behavior occurred.

2. **Behavior**

   Describe the actual, observable behavior being discussed. Don't say "you are" or "you always." Keep to the facts and avoid inserting opinions.

3. **Impact**

   Describe the impact of the behavior.

I would recommend that you also ask how the receiver experienced the situation and then offer some next steps the person can follow to improve their behavior in the future. This shows that you want to be helpful.

Here are three examples of the SBI model with the next steps:

1. During the team meeting yesterday, you interrupted your colleagues several times while they were presenting their ideas. This made it challenging for us to express our thoughts and led to a less productive discussion.
   - How did you experience the situation?
   - In our next meeting, I suggest that you try to be more mindful about making sure that everyone gets to finish their thoughts before you chime in to add value to the conversation.

2. In the customer service call yesterday, you raised your voice and became argumentative when handling the customer complaint. I think the customer might have felt unheard and dissatisfied with our service.

- How did you feel the call went?
- I know it can be hard to deal with a customer complaint, but it's important that we always treat our customers with kindness and respect, even when they don't offer us the same.

3. In the project group chat, you made sarcastic comments and criticized team members' suggestions. I felt that this discouraged open communication and collaboration and is out of line with our values.
   - Is there something going on that I should be aware of?
   - If you have issues with someone, I need you to take those directly to the person in question and do it in a respectful way.

6 **Follow up.**

If you see that the individual becomes defensive or emotional during the feedback, it's crucial to follow up. Ask, for example, "My intent was to be helpful, but I might have missed the mark. How could I have approached it differently?"

Additionally, when giving feedback that pertains to some specific area of development, it's important to have a follow-up conversation. Ask if there are ways you could provide further support to aid the person in their growth.

Three Keys to Dealing with Entrenched and Severe Behavior

In situations where the behavior is severe and the individual shows a refusal to change, despite consistent efforts to address the issue, decisive action is critical. The specific course of action may vary based on labor laws and other factors, and it should always uphold the integrity of all parties involved.

However, continuing to wait out the situation and hoping for change is ineffective and sometimes outright catastrophic. I recognize that these decisions are tough. I have personally faced situations where I made every possible rationalization to defend the behavior of a destructive leader, even when the toxic behaviors were so egregious that immediate resignation should have been the obvious course of action. Regrettably, I became complicit in covering it up.

Through extensive work with various leaders and organizations, we've learned that holding onto a person with entrenched bad behavior will often only get costlier over time.

Here are three things to consider:

1 **Don't define values you're not willing to enforce.**
When we define values and behaviors, it's crucial to ask ourselves, *Would we enforce them even if it would mean severing ties with the CEO, the top earner, the head researcher, or the top performer?* If the honest answer is no, we should not claim it as a value in our organization. Conversely, if we deal with bad behavior, even when exhibited by a high performer, it proves a strong commitment to our values.

2 **Be as transparent as you can.**

How we deal with bad behavior, especially if it includes terminating an employee, can often lead to uncertainty, rumors, and mistrust. I coach leaders to be as transparent as possible while respecting confidentiality and the individual's integrity. Concealing or fabricating stories seldom ends well.

3 **If you have disregarded bad behavior, get humble and restore trust.**

Every leader will at some point realize they have disregarded behavior they shouldn't have accepted. It's tempting to assume that this inaction hasn't had any negative side effects on the team or organization. However, that is sadly often not the case. Instead of quickly moving forward, I encourage you to revisit Practices 2 and 3. Reflect on what ways you might need to take ownership and work to repair broken trust.

As previously mentioned, the unwanted behavior we disregard has an uncanny tendency to spread. Dealing with unwanted behavior is uncomfortable, but avoiding it is seldom worth the price. Being a values-driven leader means we are ready to undertake difficult conversations because we truly care about our team members, the health of our culture, and the mission of our organization.

You Can Culture   Month 6

Reflection
- What unhelpful or destructive behaviors have you been tolerating or condoning?
- What might have kept you from addressing them effectively?
- How could you begin to address them in a caring and more effective way?

Action
- Commit to implement one specific change to more intentionally deal with unhelpful or destructive behavior in a caring, humble, and direct way. Consider the changes and challenges you observe over time.

The Practice at a Glance
Unchecked, unhelpful, or destructive behavior, especially when demonstrated by high performers, tends to spread. To cultivate cultural health, we must give caring, humble, and direct feedback and be consistent and transparent in dealing with unhelpful or destructive behavior. We must pledge to only communicate values we are truly committed to adhere to even when it gets costly.

" While the cost of dealing with unhelpful or destructive behavior might seem substantial, the cost of inaction is often considerably higher. "

Further Resources

Books:

- *Difficult Conversations: How to Discuss What Matters Most* by Douglas Stone, Bruce Patton, and Sheila Heen
- *Radical Candor: How to Get What You Want by Saying What You Mean* by Kim Scott

Podcasts:

- "Building a Culture of Compassionate Candor"—my interview with Kim Scott on the *Leading Transformational Change* podcast
- "What It Takes to Build a Remarkable Culture—Learnings from the World's Largest Culture Study"—my interview with Charlie Sull on the *Leading Transformational Change* podcast

VISIT **YOUCANCULTURE.COM**
FOR MORE RESOURCES.

Habit 3

Get Listening

Leaders who refuse to listen will eventually be surrounded by people who have nothing significant to say.[1]

—Author Andy Stanley

12

A Charlatan, the Nobel Prize, and a Defiant Hospital

Karl-Henrik Grinnemo never anticipated becoming a whistle-blower. As a cardiothoracic surgeon at Karolinska University Hospital in Stockholm and a postdoc at Karolinska Institute (the university responsible for selecting the Nobel Prize in medicine), he was on an impressive career trajectory in a field he loved. However, his life would take a dramatic turn.

In 2011 Grinnemo witnessed a medical breakthrough, or so he thought, at least.[1] Karolinska hired Paolo Macchiarini, a charismatic visiting professor and a renowned surgeon, to enhance the hospital's international standing through his purportedly groundbreaking research in regenerative medicine using synthetic windpipes. When Macchiarini first implanted a windpipe in a patient suffering from tracheal cancer at Karolinska, Grinnemo felt honored to be a part of the surgery team. He also played a minor role in the second surgery, but he remained unaware about the patients' outcomes, as they were sent to other countries for continued treatment. However, when he witnessed the severe complications of the third patient, Grinnemo realized something was seriously wrong.

Along with three colleagues who shared his concern, he decided to look into the research. As they began digging, they realized that Macchiarini had not been transparent about the outcomes of earlier windpipe surgeries and that crucial aspects of his research were based on deceptive claims. Recognizing the challenge of confronting a superstar like Macchiarini backed by Karolinska's leadership, they diligently gathered and verified evidence over many months. In 2014, feeling they had an airtight case, they presented it to leadership.

Grinnemo told me, in a 2022 interview, that it initially seemed like the vice chancellor took their concerns seriously.[2] But then leadership turned silent and refrained from taking any action. Instructed to file an official complaint, Grinnemo and his colleagues invested more time in preparing and submitting it, only to be met with further silence. Instead of addressing Macchiarini, Karolinska's leadership made life difficult for Grinnemo and even threatened to terminate his employment. He was shunned by his colleagues and overlooked for opportunities—a dark chapter that took a significant toll on him personally and negatively affected his family.

Eventually, information leaked, leading to critical articles in the *New York Times* and *Vanity Fair*,[3] as well as a documentary on Swedish television. Karolinska finally investigated and acknowledged Macchiarini's misconduct. Tragically, all three patients died after enduring harrowing complications.

Grinnemo told me that any university could hire a fraudulent researcher by mistake. However, if Karolinska's leadership had chosen to solicit, listen, and act on feedback and concerns, they could have set an example for decisively addressing research misconduct.

Instead, their reluctance to listen resulted in an internationally tarnished reputation and a crisis of trust.

In 2016, Grinnemo and his colleagues received a whistleblower award from Transparency International for their courage in speaking up.[4]

I asked Grinnemo whether he regretted the decision to speak up, considering all the pain it caused him. He said he didn't. Witnessing the patients' suffering, he believed there was no other option. He would make the same choice again.

What Gets Lost in Silence

High on the list of life's regrets is often our failure to speak up when we should have. For many years after leaving the destructive cult I grew up in, I frequently dreamed of challenging the senior leader and advocating for those mistreated instead of becoming complicit in the actions. Sadly, in reality, I mostly remained silent when I should have spoken up. It wasn't until the end of my time there that I summoned the courage to become more outspoken.

On the flip side, choosing to speak up in crucial moments defines our values and character. Darden Business School professor Jim Detert, author of *Choosing Courage*, has spent two decades researching courage in the workplace. He told me, in a 2021 interview, that if you ask people to look back at their regrets, "They are more likely to feel guilt over times they could have and should have stood up and defended someone and didn't than they are over saying, 'Oh I tried it, and it failed.'"[5]

Cultural issues often crop up when people don't speak up

about early warning signs or they do say something but are left unheard. Mary Inman, a leading whistleblower lawyer, found that about 80 percent of whistleblowers spoke up internally, often several times, before they turned to external parties.[6] They decided to go to the media or regulators, she told me in a 2021 interview, because of their frustration with how the issue was swept under the rug instead of being adequately addressed.

> *To transform our cultural health and mitigate cultural issues, we must cultivate an environment where people feel safe to speak up because cultural health deteriorates in silence.*

When our culture becomes silent, we lose:

- suggestions of improvements,
- new initiatives and innovation,
- a diversity of perspectives,
- lessons from mistakes,
- an awareness of values dilemmas, and
- concerns and warnings about unethical behavior and compliance risks.

While the antidote to silence is people speaking up, it's often a lot harder to do than we realize. Thus, we have to get listening and recognize that listening takes intentionality and creativity. That's what we'll be exploring in Habit 3.

The Habit at a Glance
Q3

When team members don't speak up or their voices go unheard, we lose critical insight into dilemmas, concerns, and opportunities for learning, improvement, and growth. As leaders, we often over-estimate our listening ability and underestimate how hard it can be to give feedback or raise concerns. To break the silence, transform our cultural health, and avoid pitfalls, we must get listening by soliciting feedback, creating conditions for brave conversations, and exercising voicing our values.

Practices to Get Listening

In this quarter, we will explore the following three monthly practices to help transform your cultural health.

Practice 7: Solicit Feedback and Break the Silence

Recognizing that speaking up is often much more challenging than we assume, we must actively solicit feedback to break the silence, asking people where, not if, we fall short of our mission and values. It starts by understanding how our power might silence others and how internal objections prevent people from speaking up.

Practice 8: Create Conditions for Brave Conversations

Why do some team members remain silent during crucial discussions? It's easy to assume they have nothing to say, but that is often inaccurate. Adopting a meeting designer mindset and creating the right conditions for brave conversations ensures that more voices

A Charlatan, the Nobel Prize, and a Defiant Hospital   165

are heard. It increases psychological safety, minimizes gossip and misunderstandings, and strengthens cultural health and alignment.

Practice 9: Exercise Voicing Values

Providing opportunities for both ourselves and our team members to practice courage, articulating our values, and expressing concerns effectively fosters an environment where everyone can advocate for values and safeguard our cultural health, even when the pressure is on.

13

Practice 7:
Solicit Feedback and Break the Silence

A company gathered its team members from around the world in a beautiful resort on a sunny August day. I was invited to facilitate a workshop on values and speak-up culture. I began by warning them with a smile that we would go deep and it would get uncomfortable. I shared my personal journey of being part of a destructive culture and becoming complicit in psychological abuse, admitting how, despite considering myself a values-driven leader, I failed to act and speak up when it truly mattered. I expressed my regret for my past silence and complicity.

Having shared my personal story and reasons we end up in ethical tunnel vision, I asked them to reflect on times they had spoken up about concerns, how they overcame internal objections, and how it made them feel, and then share their experiences with a neighbor. Nearly everyone expressed pride in having spoken up, even if it came at a cost.

I then asked them to contemplate the opposite scenario: think of a time when you *didn't* speak up, but in hindsight, wish you did. What hindered you from speaking up? How did it make you feel?

One of the most eye-opening stories came from a senior executive. Amid Russia's invasion of Ukraine in 2022, uncertain about peace in the Nordics, he volunteered for the Swedish Home Guard. Recalling his military service in his youth, he remembered it as an environment where coarse talk and sexist, racist, and homophobic jokes were prevalent. However, he was sure the climate must be different now since his comrades would be in their forties and fifties. To his dismay, it hadn't changed. They even coined a term for it. Someone in the group would say "values time-out," then blurt out a racist or sexist remark.

The senior executive was shocked and felt very uncomfortable. He wanted to stand up and say something about the behavior but froze in the moment. Being new in the group, he wanted to fit in, so he stayed silent, a decision he now deeply regretted.

After sharing his story, I pointed out that even though he had a very successful career, extensive leadership experience, and excellent communication skills, he struggled to speak up.

The Unconventional Picture of a Culture of Silence

When you picture a culture of silence, you may imagine heavy-handed, domineering leadership or management by fear. I know what that kind of leadership looks and feels like. However, you might assume that since you don't ascribe to that kind of leadership, your team members shouldn't have any trouble speaking up. But there may be many different reasons for silence. And you might be blissfully unaware of it.

Example 1: The Exceptionally Confident Manager

She had it all figured out. The successful municipal manager had invited my colleague and me for a meeting. As soon as she started talking, it was clear that the reason for the invitation wasn't to solicit our advice but to prove that she had cracked the code of organizational culture. With two of her team members in the room, she drew a management model on the whiteboard and made the case that as long as they hired people who were driven to perform, had the needed competence, and understood how to get results in this specific organizational and operational context, culture would take care of itself. It's as simple as that. While intelligent and convincing in her presentation, she didn't factor at all in her model the importance of building cultural health or enabling values-driven and ethical decision-making. Watching her team members' faces, I noticed they weren't as convinced as their boss that the model was all-encompassing. One made a minor attempt at softening some of her statements. However, they clearly didn't feel comfortable questioning her certainty and unwavering conviction. Some time later, I read in the news that she had been terminated due to whistleblower concerns.

Example 2: Fear of Being the Bearer of Bad News

I had seen troubling signs of cultural issues in a nonprofit. Through conversations with a few team members and volunteers, I witnessed a growing frustration with the work environment and fears of burnout. Even though I wasn't in a position of power, I felt responsible for at least bringing up the concern with the local director, a soft-spoken man in his early thirties and a good friend. Even though I have studied the importance of speaking up and regularly need to bring up hard conversations with people in positional power, I struggled. I didn't have a job to lose, and I wasn't afraid he would get mad or lash out at me. However, I didn't want to be the bearer of bad news in a culture famous for positivity and encouragement, where most people, at least on the surface, seemed overly excited about the organization and its leadership.

Example 3: Why Didn't Anyone Tell Me?

I was shocked by my team members' responses when I asked them to complete a survey regarding their experiences with the culture, environment, and leadership at the communications agency I founded. I questioned why I hadn't detected some of the concerns and issues earlier. If these problems were genuine, why hadn't anyone informed me before? I wish I could say that my immediate reaction was one of reflection, but instead, I became defensive. I thought, "Couldn't they have just brought that up? I'm not intimidating." Instead of reflecting on the reasons behind their silence, my initial instinct was to prove them wrong.

I believe the leaders in all three examples expected their team members to have the courage to speak up if they had something to say (I know I did). Yet raising concerns was a lot harder than we assumed. Professor Jim Detert, the courage researcher, told me, "The fact that we have created contexts where so many everyday behaviors are seen as requiring courage says a lot about the kind of environments we've created. And it's not positive."[1] While putting the onus of responsibility on our team members to speak up might seem to give us a pass, it doesn't solve the issue of silence.

> *Instead of encouraging courage, we should ask ourselves why it's so hard to raise concerns and speak up and what we must do to make it easier.*

Barriers to Speaking Up

When we or our team members consider speaking up—raising a concern, a question, or a dilemma—we face several internal objections and rationalizations that might make us determine that it's better or safer to stay silent. Here are some of the most common ones (drawing from the work of Ethics Professor Mary Gentile and others[2]):

- It's not a big deal. "It's just the way things are done around here."
- It's outside of my responsibility.
- It's not going to make a difference.
- I want to be loyal to my colleague or manager.
- I'm afraid of retaliation or negative consequences.

I can identify many times when these objections and rationalizations have been central to my decision to stay silent in moments when I should have spoken up. I'm sure you might also recognize some of them in your experiences. Reflecting on these objections and rationalizations helps us understand the challenges someone faces when deciding to speak up. People may also have past experiences that have validated these objections and are hard to break. They spoke up and realized it didn't make a difference. They were told not to bother since it was "above their pay grade." They faced negative consequences, whether emotional, relational, or financial.

However, it's our job as leaders to break through anyway. To do that, we need to reflect on what it means to have power.

While we might assume we are approachable and nonthreatening, research shows[3] how we often overestimate our listening ability and underestimate how scary it may feel to give feedback and raise concerns. Professor Megan Reitz, coauthor of *Speak Up* who has spent the last two decades researching how to create a culture of listening and speaking up, told me that "most leaders don't realize how intimidating they are."[4] They don't see how their sources of power and privilege might lead to silence.

The most obvious form of power is positional power. I've heard leaders taking on senior positions being forewarned by their predecessors that they were about to become much funnier because employees would now begin to laugh at their mediocre jokes. Team members would tell them what they wanted to hear but not necessarily what they genuinely needed to hear. Addressing issues with someone wielding power over our job security and income is inherently intimidating.

While positional power has a significant impact, power can also come with seniority, tenure, educational level, role, etc. I've met people in support functions who hesitate to ask questions or bring concerns to certain team members due to the fear of being belittled or labeled as stupid. Or university employees who know they can't question the behavior of a distinguished professor. Or new team members who would never dare to share new and innovative ideas because they fear dismissal by the old guard in the company.

And then there's the question of privileges related to gender, ethnicity, age, physical ability, etc. While we can't influence them, we must be keenly aware of how the privileges we hold in a certain environment might silence others. Failing to do so could result in inadvertently creating a culture where certain people or groups are rarely given a voice.

It's impossible to fully understand how our power and privilege influence the people around us. Professor Megan Reitz and coauthor John Higgins suggest that we ask ourselves, "What sources of power might others perceive you to have?"[5] While we won't be able to answer that perfectly, posing the question is an important starting point.

> *It's not about trying to make yourself inferior but about being humble regarding the fact that what might seem safe to you might be risky to someone else.*

After hearing me speak on how power might silence others, a participant in one of our leadership programs told me she had an epiphany. She had never before reflected on the impact of her positional power and decided to begin integrating some simple practices to solicit feedback. It changed her approach to leadership.

Seven Keys to Soliciting Feedback and Learning

Awareness of power differentials helps us understand that relevant information and critical concerns will not automatically come to our attention. We shouldn't assume that people will walk into our office (if we have one), even though we claim that our door is always open. We must actively solicit feedback and see it as a gift, even when it's uncomfortable.

I asked Kim Scott, a former Google and YouTube executive known for her bestselling book *Radical Candor*, how leaders intentionally can get values, dilemmas, and concerns on the table. Scott said her advice is usually to praise in public and criticize in private; however, if you're the leader, "You actually want to solicit public criticism."[6] If we, as leaders, solicit public criticism and treat feedback as a gift, we will lead by example.

Here are seven keys to soliciting feedback and learning (points one through five draw inspiration from my conversation with Scott):

1 **Define go-to questions.**
   Having go-to questions to solicit feedback can make it more natural to you. Scott's go-to question is, "What could I do or stop doing that would make it easier to work with me?"[7] However, it's important that you find a question that feels natural to you.

Here are a few suggestions of questions related to culture and values:

- Where do you see me or our leadership team acting in a way that could conflict with our values?
- Every organization has areas where we say one thing but then act differently. Where do you observe such inconsistencies in my leadership or in our organization?
- Where have we departed from our values this last week/ month through our behaviors, decisions, or priorities?

- What are your concerns about our new business plan/change management plan/strategy?
- Where do you see incentives or business goals that might pressure you or others to act contrary to our values?

2 **Ask *what* and *where*, not *if*.**

You might have noticed that I used *what* and *where*, not *if* in the above questions. That's because it feels safer to object or raise a concern if it seems expected and assumed that issues exist. For example, an organization sent their team members an email about upcoming, rather painful, changes due to senior leadership misconduct. They ended the email with, "If you have any questions, please reach out to our COO." Rephrasing that sentence to, "We know you have questions, and we would love for you to send them to our COO," would convey that concerns and questions are expected and welcomed, not a nuisance.

3 **Make space for silence.**

When you've asked people uncomfortable questions, you'll be tempted to jump in immediately if you don't get a direct response. However, by instead allowing several seconds of silence, you can give people time to prepare their thoughts, signaling that you genuinely want their feedback and aren't in a rush to get to the next item on the agenda. When I've waited a few seconds for a response, I often half-jokingly say that I'm really good at awkward silences. After some laughter, someone will often venture to speak up, and others will follow suit.

4   **Say thank you.**
When people do bring up concerns or dilemmas, you must avoid becoming defensive and appreciate that they went out on a limb, even if they could have phrased it more eloquently. What they need from you is a thank-you, indicating that you appreciate their courage and contribution. It signals that speaking up is rewarded and not punished in your organization.

5   **Reconnect.**
While you might disagree with their concerns or proposed actions, you must reconnect and let them know what you've decided to do or why you decided not to act. Reconnecting helps people overcome the assumption that speaking up doesn't make a difference.

6   **Celebrate people who bring up concerns.**
What we celebrate and promote will multiply. Recognizing people who bring up concerns or dilemmas will show your team and organization that you empower dissenting voices. It might be as simple as recognizing and celebrating an employee who spoke up, like Rob Chesnut did in front of his team in Practice 5. Some organizations share stories of employees who voiced their values and illustrate how it positively impacted the organization and resulted in favorable outcomes for the employee, during the onboarding process, to communicate to new team members the value of speaking up.

7 Avoid destructive feedback.

Soliciting feedback is aimed at getting valuable feedback that can help improve the organization, its culture, and your leadership. Distinguishing between genuine concerns and unconstructive grievances can be challenging. It's important to avoid making quick judgments, overlooking possibly valuable feedback, and refraining from dismissing someone's feedback based on their tone or expression. In Practice 12 we will explore ways to help our team members speak up competently, including examples of feedback we can offer when someone raises a concern. However, if someone speaks up in a toxic way—for example, going on a personal attack— it's important to close the conversation and explain why that behavior is not in line with your values.

As mentioned earlier, we cannot presume that crucial information, concerns, and dilemmas will naturally come to our attention.

Given that speaking up is often more challenging than we might assume, it is essential to actively solicit feedback and make it clear to everyone that expressing their thoughts will be both encouraged and celebrated.

You Can Culture   Month 7

Reflection

- Do you consistently seek feedback from your team members regarding ways you can improve your leadership or areas for which you are responsible?
- What factors might make it difficult for your team members or peers to give you feedback?
- What could you change to solicit feedback and break the silence more intentionally?

Action

- Commit to implementing one specific change to actively solicit feedback and intentionally break the silence. Consider the changes and challenges you observe over time.

The Practice at a Glance

Recognizing that speaking up is often much more challenging than we assume, we must actively solicit feedback to break the silence, asking people where, not if, we fall short of our mission and values. It starts by understanding how our power might silence others and how internal objections prevent people from speaking up.

> *While we might assume we are approachable and nonthreatening, we often overestimate our listening ability and underestimate how scary it may feel to give feedback and raise concerns.*

Further Resources

Books:

- *Speak Up: Say What Needs to Be Said and Hear What Needs to Be Heard* by Megan Reitz and John Higgins

Podcasts:

- "A Culture of Speaking Up and Listening Up"—my interview with Megan Reitz on the *Leading Transformational Change* podcast
- "Building a Culture of Compassionate Candor"—my interview with Kim Scott on the *Leading Transformational Change* podcast
- "Learnings from a Whistleblower"—my interview with Bianca Goodson and Mary Inman on the *Leading Transformational Change* podcast

VISIT **YOUCANCULTURE.COM**
FOR MORE RESOURCES.

14

Practice 8:
Create Conditions for
Brave Conversations

The information hit the multinational company like a bomb. The president and founder had abruptly resigned due to misconduct. Rumors were spreading in the media and left the organization reeling with uncertainty. In an effort to address the situation, one of the regional leaders convened a Zoom call with seventy top team members. He talked for a while and ended by asking if anyone had a question, but despite the gravity of the situation, he was met with silence.

Later, the leader confided that he believed people must have had a lot of questions, yet no one volunteered. I have heard similar stories numerous times—leaders struggling to initiate conversations despite knowing their team members have a lot of opinions.

We might mistakenly assume that our team has nothing to say, but often the core problem is a failure to create conducive conditions for sharing their views and input.

In many cases, the conversations move to inappropriate forums, where we won't be there to hear or address them. As the British bestselling artist Adele would say, "Rumor has it."

Leaders tend to focus on giving presentations and speeches in team meetings but often neglect planning for courageous, vulnerable, and authentic discussions. A prevailing excuse, in my experience, is that we're busy and don't feel like we have the time. However, if we are to cultivate and sustain cultural health, we need to ensure to seek out important ideas, diverse perspectives, lessons from mistakes, questions, and concerns.

Failing to create conditions for brave conversations often results in spending precious time and energy dealing with rumors, gossip, misunderstandings, mistrust, and a lack of clarity.

We have leaders and team members seemingly agreeing in the meeting but then disagreeing and taking disparate actions as soon as the meeting ends. I'm sure you've experienced how frustrating that can be. This discrepancy will hinder needed commitment and impede progress, especially when navigating through organizational change.

Let's redesign the conversation in the example I gave before. The leader had time to prepare his remarks, but his colleagues didn't. Instead of asking for instant feedback, it would have been advisable to say, "I know that you have important questions. Let's take five minutes to write them down. I'll then invite each of you to share your questions, addressing as many as possible in this call. We'll schedule a follow-up meeting to address any additional questions." Or even better, give people a chance to write their questions on a digital whiteboard and then schedule a separate meeting the day after to address them. These minor changes would have made it safer to bring up concerns and would most surely have yielded a different result.

Psychological Safety Matters

What makes a team effective at Google? That was the million-dollar question Google, the global tech giant, tried to answer through a research effort named Project Aristotle in 2015. The study has since become famous, mostly because of their surprising findings. The research team assumed that effectiveness primarily had to do with getting the right mix of brilliant individuals on the team. However, they found that "who is on a team matters less than how the team members interact, structure their work, and view their contributions." The resulting study detailed five keys to a successful Google team. On top of the list, and what they realized was the linchpin of the other four keys, was psychological safety. They chose to define it as, "Team members feel safe to take risks and be vulnerable in front of each other."[1]

While the concept of psychological safety dates back to research in the 1950s, it saw a revival through the research and writings of Harvard Business School professor Amy Edmondson. Edmondson was, in 1999, researching the effect of teamwork on medical error rates.[2] She hypothesized that the data would show that the most effective teams would have the least errors. However, she found something surprising. The teams where the members felt safe speaking openly about mistakes and risk of errors were also the ones who performed the least errors.

According to Timothy R. Clark, the author of *The 4 Stages of Psychological Safety*, psychological safety "is a condition in which you feel (1) included, (2) safe to learn, (3) safe to contribute, and (4) safe to challenge the status quo—all without fear of being embarrassed, marginalized, or punished in some way."[3]

Working with leaders and teams on every level, I've often observed that a lack of psychological safety impairs their ability to successfully drive necessary change. I've seen that lack in start-ups and in large organizations alike. I've seen it in the executive suite and on the factory floor. People don't share their mistakes, bring their best ideas or relevant dilemmas, ask important questions, and challenge one another. They aren't willing to question how things are done.

Organizations are, of course, not all the same, and in a highly regulated and standardized environment, leaders might not necessarily need or even want people to spend too much time taking risks and suggesting new ways of doing things. However, I have yet to meet an organization or a team that wouldn't benefit from fostering an environment where people feel safe being vulnerable, sharing lessons learned from mistakes, contributing ideas for improvement, and speaking up about concerns or risks.

A lack of psychological safety has, as we've seen throughout this book, serious implications for the organization's ability to effectively deliver on its mission, build a thriving workplace, and have a responsible impact.

It's important to note that psychological safety is a group-level phenomenon, so there's much you can do to foster it within your team, even though it might not be a strong trait throughout the broader organization. Psychological safety holds significance in all types of collaboration, but its discernible impact, whether present or absent, becomes particularly pronounced during meetings.

Think like a Meeting Designer

I remember this meeting like it was yesterday. I was helping the executive team of a multinational organization address a breakdown of trust and lead through a very delicate culture change process. As leaders were bravely and vulnerably sharing their perspectives of what had led to the breakdown, a longtime board member, who had never engaged in the process before, dismissed it as a waste of time and a diversion from the critical mission. The atmosphere became so tense that you could practically cut it with a knife. Despite this, I thanked him for his input and steered the meeting forward. Thankfully, due to weeks of intentional efforts in fostering a psychologically safe environment within the group, the rest of the executive team chose to press on, undeterred by his remarks.

While tensions might sometimes run high in both your work environment and mine, I think few of us face the kind of high-stakes meetings that Adam Kahane has made his life's work. Kahane, the author of *Collaborating with the Enemy*, is an expert at bringing people with conflicting interests together to solve critical problems. Juan Manuel Santos, former Colombian president and Nobel Peace Prize recipient, credits Kahane's work with playing a pivotal role in the process of bringing the fifty-year-long Colombian civil war to an end by helping facilitate meetings and collaboration between the government, the FARC guerrilla, and other stakeholders.[4]

Kahane told me, in a 2021 interview, he believes it's possible, and many times necessary, to collaborate with people we do not agree with. However, the participants have to feel safe that (1) they can contribute with their diverse perspectives, (2) they can connect to one another and to the motivation behind their participation, and (3) they can contribute in an equitable and fair manner.[5] I think that every leader can take a page from Kahane and the idea that if it's possible to even get sworn enemies into a conversation, we can all create better conditions for brave conversations in our meetings.

However, we might need to change the way we view our role in the meeting. Instead of identifying solely as meeting leaders, we need to see ourselves as meeting designers. Fred Dust, a former global managing partner at the iconic design firm IDEO and author of *Making Conversation*, who has extensive experience designing dialogues for problem-solving in governments and large organizations, told me in a 2022 interview that he believes every leader can and should take on the role of a meeting designer.

> "There are new possibilities if you can begin to think about how you influence the structure and feel of a conversation by design rather than by pure force of will. It relies not on your interpersonal skills but a different skill set: the ability to spot opportunity and design for it in order to shape outcome and impact."[6]

To begin the design process, you should determine objectives and reflect on enablers and possible obstacles. I recommend that you ask yourself four simple questions:

1. What do you want this conversation/meeting to accomplish?
2. How would you like the participants to contribute?
3. What might hinder the participants from contributing effectively?
4. What might enable them to contribute effectively?

When you've asked those four questions and set some objectives, the next question then becomes, how could you design the conversation to help accomplish those goals? And that's what we'll look at next. But by merely taking two minutes to ask yourself the above questions, you will take a major step toward better conversations.

Eight Keys to Creating Conditions for Brave Conversations

We've so far discussed the need to take on the role of designer and begin by setting the appropriate objectives. Here are eight other keys to creating the right conditions for brave conversations in a psychologically safe environment.

1 **Show up intentionally.**
If we show up stressed and distracted, chances are other people will also feel the same way. Putting away other tasks and dedicating even just two to three minutes before the start of the meeting to reflect on the meeting objectives will help you show up present and ready for the conversation.

2 **Start with a check-in.**
The other participants will likely enter the conversation with a hundred different thoughts and pressures on their mind. A brief check-in can offer them an opportunity to set aside distractions and be fully present. A simple question to ask is, what do you need to put aside to be fully present in this meeting? However, keep it short.

3   Set rules for devices.

We've all experienced those meetings where certain individuals persistently check their digital devices. It communicates to the other participants that their contribution isn't important, making them feel unproductive or undervalued and prompting them to check their devices as well. I usually ask participants if we can agree to put phones and computers away, unless we're taking notes or receiving a pressing call from a family member or client. Establishing this rule at the onset makes it less awkward to point out when people break it.

4   Agree on shared principles.

Establish a few shared principles for the meeting. For example: In this meeting it's OK to (1) be vulnerable, (2) ask questions and say that you don't understand, (3) encourage people who haven't shared their perspective to speak up, (4) ask someone to further explain their point of view, (5) kindly raise the need to get back to the main topic of the meeting, (6) address concerns that come up, and (7) ask for more time to address an important issue. However, it's *not* OK to (1) belittle someone else's contribution, (2) talk over other participants, and (3) take time from other people without asking for permission. Once these principles are agreed upon, it becomes essential to gently point out when people break them. This fosters a culture of mutual respect and ensures the meeting stays aligned with its intended purpose.

5 Set the tone.

I've pointed this out several times already. By demonstrating humility and vulnerability through, for example, asking questions or sharing a mistake or a struggle, you will make it much more likely that others will feel safe to do the same. Be intentional about how you demonstrate humility and set the right tone.

6 Include everyone's perspective strategically.

Some people are quick to jump into a conversation and share their views, while others need time to think and reflect before they're ready to contribute. Some will unconsciously dominate the conversation, while others have no trouble sitting silently through a meeting.

To promote more equal participation, I often let attendees take a few minutes to write down their reflections on an issue before I go around the table asking for everyone's perspective. In larger groups, it can be helpful to break into smaller groups of three to four people and have them agree on their perspective and then share it with the larger group. Moreover, getting the participants' consent to allow the facilitator (or meeting chair) to call on people who haven't spoken yet and politely interrupt those who have taken a lot of time helps ensure a balanced conversation.

7 Sift for disagreement.

If you suspect there are opposing views that haven't been shared, it can be helpful to ask specifically for dissenting viewpoints. For example, what are your concerns with this idea? What would a dissenting view be? Employing simple tricks can also be beneficial. A helpful exercise I use to sift for disagreement is the "stinky fish" exercise.

The stinky fish is a metaphor for a concern or anxiety—"that thing that you carry around but don't like to talk about, but the longer you hide it, the stinkier it gets."[7] In this exercise, participants are given a printed or digital image of a stinky fish and are asked to write down their fears or concerns related to, for example, a new change initiative. Afterward, everyone shares their "stinky fish," and they address the concerns one by one. Using a metaphor that might seem a bit silly helps make it more acceptable and safer to share serious concerns.

8   **Rotate the responsibility to chair meetings.**
Rotating the responsibility to chair, for example, a recurring team meeting can enhance equity and foster a greater sense of ownership for the meeting objectives among team members.

Creating conditions for brave conversations will help us greatly improve the output of our meetings and ensure we get critical information on the table.

You Can Culture   Month 8

Reflection

- How would your team members, in your perception, rate the level of psychological safety in your meetings on a scale of one to ten?
- How might the way you typically design your meetings or conversations promote or hinder participation and brave conversations?
- How could implementing the thinking of a meeting designer help ensure that all voices are heard?

Action

- Commit to implementing one specific change to the design of your team meetings to create better conditions for brave conversations. Consider the changes and challenges you observe over time.

The Practice at a Glance

Why do some team members remain silent during crucial discussions? It's easy to assume they have nothing to say, but that is often inaccurate. Adopting a meeting designer mindset and creating the right conditions for brave conversations ensures that more voices are heard. It increases psychological safety, minimizes gossip and misunderstandings, and strengthens cultural health and alignment.

"*We might mistakenly assume that our team has nothing to say, but often the core problem is a failure to create conducive conditions for sharing their views and input.* "

Further Resources

Books:

- *The Fearless Organization: Creating Psychological Safety in the Workplace for Learning, Innovation, and Growth* by Amy C. Edmondson
- *The 4 Stages of Psychological Safety: Defining the Path to Inclusion and Innovation* by Timothy R. Clark
- *Making Conversation: Seven Essential Elements of Meaningful Communication* by Fred Dust
- *Facilitating Breakthrough: How to Remove Obstacles, Bridge Differences, and Move Forward Together* by Adam Kahane

Podcasts:

- "Designing Hard Conversations to Solve Big Problems"—my interview with Fred Dust on the *Leading Transformational Change* podcast
- "Bridge Difference and Facilitate Breakthrough"—my interview with Adam Kahane on the *Leading Transformational Change* podcast
- "Creating a Culture of Responsible Leadership at a Multinational Medtech-Company"—my interview with Michaela Ahlberg and Anna Romberg on the *Leading Transformational Change* podcast

VISIT **YOUCANCULTURE.COM**
FOR MORE RESOURCES.

15

Practice 9:
Exercise Voicing Values

It was a crisis of faith for Professor Mary Gentile. As Enron and other high-profile corporate scandals were thrust into the spotlight, she found students from leading business schools in front-page news, accused of severe corporate misconduct. It added to her feeling that the way ethics was often taught was futile or hypocritical at worst, and she felt compelled to understand what had gone wrong.

Gentile had been part of designing and teaching the first required ethics curriculum at Harvard Business School. After ten years at Harvard, she went on to help other leading business universities implement their ethics training. The typical curriculum was aimed at providing students with a decision-making framework to help them identify ethical issues that might come up, consider different philosophical models such as virtue ethics or utilitarianism, and then determine the appropriate course of action. The problem was that students got stuck in theory. They could go through the entire curriculum and still not know what to do when facing real ethical issues at their workplaces.

You've probably had a similar realization as Gentile did—that merely reading a list of values or offering training on your code of conduct doesn't by itself empower and equip someone to act and speak up, even when they know what is right. They might still end up freezing in the moment, like I've done many times myself.

Gentile told me, in a 2020 interview, that as she was facing her crisis of faith, she started seeing an increasing amount of research in psychology, neuroscience, and other fields, suggesting that to change people's behavior, allowing them to pre-script and rehearse how to voice and act on their values with peers might be more effective than teaching them ethical frameworks.[1] The "aha" moment came when she attended a self-defense class that taught model mugging.[2] As in any self-defense class, they would learn physical moves to use if attacked. However, as they began to master the moves, all the students would line up, and a man in a padded suit would attack them one by one, allowing them to practice the moves they had learned. Gentile told me that it felt ludicrous at first as they stood around waiting to be attacked. However, as they grew more confident, the strategy changed. Now the man in the suit would show up when they were focused on other things and attack them without warning. Gentile found it nerve-racking, never knowing when or how the attack would occur. However, the idea was that if you practiced something in the same physiological, cognitive, and emotional state as in a real-life attack, your body would develop muscle memory and remember the moves even if you froze in the moment.

One day, as Gentile was lying on the floor after having failed to protect herself from the man in the padded suit, she had an epiphany.

What if you could develop moral muscle memory?

A default and informed behavior that would come almost automatically when you faced ethical dilemmas or values conflict, helping you act on and give voice to your values confidently and competently. That would change everything. This led Gentile to create the Giving Voice to Values curriculum, now used at about 1,500 business schools and companies,[3] to help people practice speaking up and giving voice to their values so that they would be better equipped to face ethical challenges in the workplace.

Developing the Skills of Voicing Values and Speaking Up

Listening to numerous examples of values conflicts and ethical dilemmas, I've noticed that some people were more strategic about speaking up, leading to a greater sense of pride over their decision to act (regardless of the outcome). In contrast, others felt like they froze in the moment and failed to raise the issue effectively—an experience that left them frustrated or disappointed. I make a distinction here between giving critical or corrective feedback, as we discussed in Practice 6, and speaking up about a concern or dilemma to someone with some form of power over us.

Speaking up competently inside an organization means that someone presents their issue or concern in a way that has the greatest chance of leading to a positive outcome.

It's acting in the organization's best interest and not merely out of self-interest. It's less about calling out as an outside observer and more about speaking up as someone who truly cares about the organization's success and the well-being of its employees, clients, and other stakeholders.

I encourage you to stop and reflect for a moment on times when you've spoken up, whether to a superior, a client, or someone else with either formal or informal power. You can probably identify times you did it competently and other times you failed to do so.

In the best experiences I have had, I managed to stay cool, build a compelling case, and use my communication skills and the trust that I had built with the person or the organization in question to present my case in a winsome way. In the worst situations, I was too emotional and frustrated about the situation and wasn't able to be levelheaded and professional, which unfortunately lessened my effectiveness and made it easier for the receiver to disregard my opinion (even when they had a duty to act).

Professor Jim Detert's extensive research into workplace courage offers some helpful tips on what it takes to speak up competently.[4]

1. Create the right conditions by being a person who builds trust and a good reputation within the organization.
2. Choose your battles wisely and speak up about things that truly matter to you (which requires you to get clear on your personal and organizational values and regularly spend time reflecting on them as we've discussed in Practices 1 and 4).
3. Be intentional about the message by, for example, avoiding calling people out as unethical and instead asking questions such as, "I'm wondering if this is consistent with our values? I'm wondering if this is the industry standard? Have you discussed this with others inside or outside the company?"

---

4. Channel your emotions by, for example, trying to stay cool and composed.
5. Take action after the act by following up and, if possible, helping ensure a positive outcome.

I've asked hundreds of managers to rate how skilled they believe their team members are at competently raising concerns and issues. Most of the time, the results are dismal. Many managers share with me their frustration that their team members voice concerns in a way that isn't competent or constructive and that sometimes even turns destructive.

While I believe the issue of silence is more prevalent than the problem of people speaking up too much or in the wrong way, it's vital that everyone in our organizations knows how to do it competently.

However, as Detert told me, "No one is born competently courageous."[5] Competence only improves through practice. As leaders, it's our responsibility to practice and provide opportunities for our team members to do the same.

Moving Forward through Rescripting Our Past

At the outset of the more than seven-year-long journey of crafting and refining this book, I recognized the necessity of confronting my personal narrative.

A few months earlier, I had finally delved into my mom's account of her time in the religious community that turned into a cult. After requesting a copy of her book, I received a signed one my mom had kept for years, hoping that I'd one day be prepared to read it. That day had finally arrived.

As I immersed myself in the book, memories I sought to shield myself from surged back with vivid intensity. The illusion I had cultivated, convincing myself that "it wasn't all that bad," shattered. I distinctly recalled the psychological isolation and degradation we imposed on others. I relived the fear and the sense of being ensnared in a reality I desperately wanted to escape.

While I had become increasingly vocal about my concerns in my later years in the community, I hadn't clearly communicated to the leadership why I left. I just disappeared.

Now I felt compelled to speak up to those still in power.

With my wife's support, I penned a letter to the community's board. My aim wasn't to absolve myself of guilt but to take responsibility and reflect on decisions I should have made a decade earlier, as I witnessed the investigative television program exposing the destructive culture and psychological abuse (which I shared about in the introduction).

I decided to write with a professional tone and avoid emotional language. I began by outlining the severity of the abuse, dispelling the notion that we somehow were driven by noble intentions, and emphasizing why I should have sought the founder's resignation and called for external assistance to assess and transform the culture. I highlighted how the culture of fear, silence, and the absence of important checks and balances kept us from doing what was right.

I sent the letter to the founder and other board members, and even though I had left years ago, I felt trepidation, having never articulated such a direct challenge before. I didn't anticipate it would bring about change, and as expected, I never got a response. However, little did I know how much it would come to mean to me personally.

Writing and sending the letter offered moral clarity on long-unresolved issues and helped me overcome some of my rationalizations and fear of speaking up.

I have later heard from others who left the community that reading my letter helped them gain moral clarity as well. It remains a defining moment in my life.

However, it wasn't until later that I encountered the work of Professor Mary Gentile and learned that what I did was rescripting a past experience of a values conflict—a powerful strategy to build moral muscle memory and practice giving voice to our values.[6]

While I might have wished I would never need to draw on that experience or face another need to speak up in my life, I've since learned to embrace the reality that speaking up and voicing values are just a natural part of life. Therefore, I have better get as comfortable and competent as I possibly can.

I implore you to do the same—because the reality is we can't predict when we might need it and how much it is going to matter when the situation appears.

Four Ways to Exercise Speaking Up with Your Team

In the two earlier practices in Habit 3, we've explored ways that we as leaders can help create a culture where people feel safe and encouraged to raise concerns, bring ideas to the table, and speak up. But as we've learned in this practice, we also need to exercise the ability to voice our values effectively.

Here are four ways you and your team can exercise speaking up.

1 **Follow up when soliciting feedback.**

In Practice 7, I talked about the importance of soliciting feedback. After we've clearly shown that the input is welcomed and appreciated, there might be an opportunity to provide some added feedback to help the person develop their competence and ensure that the right course of action is taken.

Here are six examples of what that might look like:

1. Thank you for sharing this concern with me! Have you brought this up with Landon, who oversees the relevant department? I believe he would love to get your feedback on this.

2. Thank you for bringing up this issue! It definitely sounds like something we should address. Do you have any advice or suggestions on how we could best approach this issue, or is there someone else you think we should talk to? Your insights could be valuable in finding a solution.

3. Thank you for bringing up this concern with me. I understand that discussing it directly with the person involved might be challenging, however, I can only address it if we engage this person in the conversation as well. I'm here to support you if you'd like to have a conversation together to ensure that you feel safe and respected.

---

4. Thank you for talking to me about this issue. I think it would be wise to bring it up with our CEO, as you suggested. Can I share some things I've learned about addressing issues with her effectively?
5. Thank you for sharing your concerns. Would you be able to give me some practical examples for me to better understand and be able to address the issue?
6. I appreciate your willingness to speak up! Your insights are valuable! Have you considered submitting a formal suggestion or proposal to our feedback system? It would help ensure the relevant teams officially document and consider your ideas.

2 Practice using values conflicts.

To practice giving voice to values as a team, you can use values conflicts to spark conversations and reflections, focusing on situations where the protagonist knows what is right and pre-scripting[7] together, as a team, how they could speak up about the situation skillfully. This includes asking questions such as: How should the protagonist best raise this concern with her boss? What might hinder her? What might enable her?

3 Rescript past experiences.

Another way to practice voicing our values is to reflect on times when we did speak up and other times when we turned silent and what differed between those two experiences. Our team has done this exercise with hundreds of people. I've often been taken aback by the depth of conversations and insights that emerge, especially when leaders are willing to be vulnerable and openly share their experiences. Professor

Mary Gentile calls the exercise "The Tale of Two Stories." A detailed description is available for free from Darden School of Business at the University of Virginia: store.darden. virginia.edu/exercise-a-tale-of-two-stories.

4   **Create support systems.**
Since speaking up is hard and it can seem embarrassing or scary to ask for advice, it helps to designate a group of people within the organization who could provide competent guidance on the matter. As the chief ethics officer at Airbnb, Rob Chesnut selected a group of ethics advisers that team members could approach to discuss values conflicts. The ethics advisers would then counsel on how to competently bring up the issues with their managers. Chesnut told me that offering this support system led to more valuable concerns and dilemmas being brought to leadership's attention.[8] We've heard from clients who have integrated a similar approach and found it very helpful.

Finally, if we get listening by making a practice of soliciting feedback, intentionally creating the right conditions for brave conversations, and offering opportunities for our team to exercise voicing their values, we will create a culture of listening and be much more likely to identify dilemmas, concerns, and important learnings as early as possible. It will help improve our leadership and our organization and avoid unnecessary negative, or even devastating, consequences.

Because cultural health deteriorates in silence.

You Can Culture

You Can Culture   Month 9

Reflection

- How competent and effective at raising concerns and voicing values would you rate yourself on a scale of one to ten?
- How competent and effective at raising concerns and voicing values would you rate your team on a scale of one to ten?
- Reflect on a situation where you, in hindsight, believe you should have spoken up or raised concerns but chose to be silent. How could you have overcome your objections and rationalizations and spoken up competently to create the best conditions for a positive outcome?

Action

- Commit to making one effort to help you and your team exercise voicing values and speaking up more effectively. For example, try rescripting a personal experience and then creating opportunities for your team to do the same. Consider the changes and challenges you observe over time.

The Practice at a Glance

Providing opportunities for both us and our team members to practice courage, articulating our values, and expressing concerns effectively fosters an environment where everyone can advocate for values and safeguard our cultural health, even when the pressure is on.

Practice 9: Exercise Voicing Values   205

" *Speaking up competently inside an organization means that someone presents their issue or concern in a way that has the greatest chance of leading to a positive outcome.* "

Further Resources

Books:

- *Giving Voice to Values: How to Speak Your Mind When You Know What's Right* by Mary C. Gentile
- *Choosing Courage: The Everyday Guide to Being Brave at Work* by Jim Detert

Podcasts:

- "Giving Voice to Values"—my interview with Mary C. Gentile on the *Leading Transformational Change* podcast
- "Choosing Courage"—my interview with Jim Detert on the *Leading Transformational Change* podcast

VISIT **YOUCANCULTURE.COM**
FOR MORE RESOURCES.

Habit 4
Get Integrity

*Integrity is choosing courage over comfort;
it's choosing what's right over what's
fun, fast, or easy; and it's practicing your
values, not just professing them.[1]*

—Author and Research Professor Brené Brown

16

One Company's Unlikely Quest to Live Their Values

The catalyst was an astounding question in 2007: "What is the right level of profit?"[1] For a shareholder of a multinational corporation, the expected answer would typically be "as much as is legally possible." However, when John Mars—shareholder and then-chairman of family-owned Mars Inc.—asked this question, he wasn't after the expected answer. Instead, he wanted the $40 billion confectionery and pet care giant's executive team to explore the question's moral and business implications. And so they did, under the leadership of Mars chief economist Bruno Roche.

As I explained in Practice 4, values cannot give us all the answers. However, they should help us wrestle with vital questions about priorities, decisions, and behaviors. While the question John Mars had raised was new, it sprung from one of Mars's original values.

In 1947, with much of Europe in ruins after the end of World War II, Forrest Mars, the son of Mars's founder, penned a business manifesto titled "The Company's Objective." It stated that the company should seek to create mutual benefit for its stakeholders, ensuring that everyone gained value from the company's activities—consumers, distributors, competitors, suppliers, governmental bodies, employees, and shareholders.[2] Mutuality became part of Mars's corporate values, known as The Five Principles. Victoria Mars, a former chairman of the company, said in an interview with PwC in 2018:

> "There's not a conversation I have with our associates and leaders, other corporations, government officials, or when I speak in public that doesn't weave in The Five Principles. Repeat, repeat, repeat; demonstrate, demonstrate, demonstrate The Five Principles all the time. It's so critical you don't forget about these five principles."[3]

While many organizations claim inspirational values, they often avoid keeping themselves accountable, leading to a lack of integrity. However, Bruno Roche and his team wanted to explore what it would take to truly integrate the principle of mutuality. They developed a theory—that if instead of only maximizing and measuring financial profit, a company would focus equally on maximizing social, human, and natural capital, they would build a more sustainable business and ultimately see better financial returns.[4] They then put that theory into practice through a joint research effort with the University of Oxford's Saïd Business School.

The effort began within the Wrigley chewing gum business (owned by Mars) in East Africa, with building a business in the slums outside of Nairobi, Kenya[5]—an area considered too dangerous for a multinational corporation and that lacked the structure needed for large-scale distribution. The team partnered with local

NGOs, with a network of women who wanted better-paid jobs and could leverage trust within their communities. With the help of a microfinance lender, they provided women with starting capital to buy a bike and a basket. This enabled them to become entrepreneurs, selling Wrigley products in the slums. Jay Jakub, former senior director of external research at Mars and current executive director of the Economics of Mutuality Foundation, shared with me in a 2021 interview that they went from a few sales associates at the beginning to about a thousand, and the project lifted hundreds of people out of poverty by offering superior wages.[6] At the same time, the company managed to churn out a healthy profit margin in a market it wouldn't otherwise have been able to cater to. By maximizing social capital, they were able to achieve significant financial returns.

The CEO of Royal Canin, a company that's also a part of Mars, wanted to integrate the principle further within the pet food business and focus on maximizing social and human capital. Their team contacted veterinarians and pet breeders to learn more about their challenges and discovered that one in five puppies dies after two weeks. They also realized there was a lack of research into pet mortality, so they launched a five-year study on the subject. The result was a groundbreaking product that could help reduce pet mortality. However, a leadership team with a sole focus on profit maximization would have advised against the development and the research because the market wasn't big or profitable enough for the product. But pursuing it strengthened Royal Canin's relationship and trust with its customers. The integration of mutuality is viewed as a critical ingredient in Royal Canin's extraordinary success and growth.[7]

Renowned Management Professor Colin Mayer, who collaborated with Mars on the research, shared with me, in a 2021 interview, how further integrating the principle of mutuality led to several remarkable innovations as the company began wrestling with values-based questions that challenged its operating model and processes.[8]

Bruno Roche and the team realized they needed to redesign the process of measuring impact. They created a new accounting process that would account for not only financial performance but also social, human, and natural capital. Today, these principles have spread worldwide through Economics of Mutuality, a nonprofit founded by Mars and heralded by some of the world's largest companies and most successful CEOs.

A few years ago, Mars decided to become the world's most mutual company. They keep themselves accountable by annually reporting on their impact on the environment and society through their Principles in Action Summary.[9] A July 2022 column in the *Economist* stated, "Mars Inc. gets the purpose v. profit balance right. Showy corporations should learn from the low-key, family-owned mammal-feeder."[10] They noted how Mars makes considerable investments in line with its values, like $1 billion to support sustainable initiatives, but that it doesn't want to brag about them. Competitors envy Mars for its high employee retention. The company was named one of the one hundred best places to work in 2022 by Glassdoor (based on employee reviews).[11]

While no organization is perfect, when team members see that their company walks the talk and does the hard work of maintaining integrity, people feel proud to be a part of it.

Water Quality and Cultural Integrity

On April 25, 2014, residents of Flint, Michigan, drank tap water just like they had done every day for years.[12] Unbeknownst to them, however, their drinking water had begun to become contaminated. Local government officials had decided to change the water source in an attempt to save money. A significant minority of Flint's population lives below the poverty line, making its residents extraordinarily dependent on access to fresh tap water. However, the more corrosive water caused dangerous lead from the aging pipes to seep into the water supply. The water that should refresh and reinvigorate people was now unsafe.

In my part of the world, we take safe tap water for granted. But clean water is very scarce for so much of the world's population. Unsafe water might look clean but could be contaminated and poisonous.

> Integrity derives from the Latin word *integer*, meaning whole or complete.[13] The purpose of having integrity is to ensure that what you as a leader, team, and organization think (your internal interactions), do (how the work gets done), and say (how you communicate externally) align with the mission and values you claim.

In 2013, three researchers concluded a five-year study of data from one thousand of the largest businesses in the US to investigate the value of corporate culture and values. Perhaps unsurprisingly, they failed to find any significant correlation between how often companies mention their values on their website and the performance of the organization. They chose to move forward and measure whether employees perceive that the values are lived out with integrity and not only advertised. They found that "high levels of perceived integrity are positively correlated with good outcomes, in terms of higher productivity, profitability, better industrial relations, and higher level of attractiveness to prospective job applicants."[14]

I'm sure we've all encountered leaders and organizations who promised lofty values but operated in clear conflict with them. This lack of integrity causes frustration, disappointment, and even distrust. Like a glass of water that appears clean but leaves you with a bad aftertaste, or worse, a deadly disease.

If you consider all the people who are impacted and "drink the water" of your organization—team members, clients, suppliers, communities, the environment, and other stakeholders—you realize that the quality of your water matters immensely. And as leaders, we are responsible for the water quality!

In our work, we've identified three areas that are especially crucial to supporting integrity and cultural health—our stories, our rituals, and our incentives and processes. And those are the areas we'll be exploring in the coming three practices.

The Habit at a Glance   Q4

Too often there's conflict between the values we claim and the signals we send. We might, for example, say we want teamwork but incentivize only individual performance. To avoid mixed signals, we must ensure that the stories we tell, the rituals we design, and the processes and incentives we set embody our mission and values and sustain our cultural health.

Practices to Get Integrity

In this quarter, we will explore the following three monthly practices to help transform your cultural health.

Practice 10: Share Stories That Embody Mission and Values

The stories we share can authentically embody our mission, reinforce our values, and strengthen our culture or be ineffective and even become instruments of manipulation. To improve our cultural health, we need to embrace the role of storytellers, lead by example, rethink the stories we tell, and consider the methods we employ to tell them.

Practice 11: Design Culture-Building Rituals

Every team engages in rituals where relationships are built, stories are told, priorities are set, and decisions are made. These rituals greatly impact the health of our teams and the quality of our professional relationships. To sustain cultural health, we must design culture-building rituals that foster connection and ongoing conversations about our mission, values, and behaviors.

Practice 12: Rethink Incentives and Processes for Cultural Health

Too often, there's a dissonance between the values we claim and the signals we send through our incentives and processes. To gain integrity, we must ensure that our incentives and processes don't foster dangerous tensions but instead help sustain cultural health over time. It requires committed effort and continuous adjustments.

Practice 10:
Share Stories That Embody Mission and Values

For five long years, they were strictly forbidden to celebrate on May 17. Norway was under Nazi German occupation between 1940 and 1945. The Norwegian flag was banned. Some people, such as Vidkun Quisling, a former minister of defense whose last name has since become synonymous with "traitor," chose to collaborate with the Nazis. Others bravely resisted.

When the Nazi occupation began, Anne Margrethe Strømsheim, a twenty-six-year-old woman from the town of Trondheim, immediately signed up to join the resistance. As the only female member of a group of 250 Norwegian resistance fighters, they valiantly resisted German forces for about a month at Hegra Fortress. Outnumbered and outgunned, they held their ground until they were forced to surrender due to overwhelming German firepower and a lack of reinforcements. Strømsheim became nationally known as a resistance heroine and was given the honorary nickname *Lotten fra Hegra*.[1]

She was decorated with several war medals, including one from the Americans.

On May 17, 1814, King Christian Fredrik signed the Norwegian constitution, declaring Norway an independent kingdom. Since the Nazi occupation, the day has taken on even more meaning. On this day, they remember people like Strømsheim, who sacrificed to protect their country's freedom. The young and old get out on the streets, dressed in national garb in the colors of the Norwegian flag. You can hear children singing the national anthem: "Yes, we love this country."

Almost every country in the world marks a national holiday where its founding or independence is celebrated. Independence days are steeped in stories of victors and losers, heroes and villains, stories that have been told and retold for generations that have helped define the group and shaped culture. When people aim to bring societal change, they often must challenge and reframe some of the stories that have been told and believed for decades or centuries.

Stories remind us of who we are and who we aspire to be. Author Sue Monk Kidd puts it beautifully in *The Secret Life of Bees*: "Stories have to be told or they die, and when they die, we can't remember who we are or why we're here."[2] Stories are compelling because we instinctively recognize and identify with the narrative of heroes and villains.

In compelling stories, the protagonist faces obstacles that must be overcome and experiences some form of transformation along a tension-filled journey toward ultimate success and/or learning from tragedy.

Just as these stories shape the narrative and culture of a nation, stories play a critical role in shaping and reinforcing the culture and values of our organizations.

Professor Jennifer Chatman at Berkeley told me that to understand an organization's culture, you should look for "the stories of success."[3]

Let's look at a few examples of stories of success that have shaped culture at some well-known organizations.

- Stories of the late IKEA founder, Ingvar Kamprad, driving an old Volvo and helping organize shopping carts at IKEA furniture stores reinforce the values of cost-consciousness and simplicity and paint executive excesses as the enemy.
- The story of Arianna Huffington—cofounder of *HuffPost* who collapsed from exhaustion and burnout, leading her to prioritize sleep and wellness in her own life and founding Thrive Global to advocate for it in the workplace—reinforces the values of employee well-being and work-life balance.
- The story of an Airbnb host having her apartment trashed by a guest in the company's early days and the executive team deciding that the company would pay up, despite not having any legal obligation, communicates the value of doing the right thing even when it's costly.

Our stories of success can carry assumptions and values that are both helpful and harmful. I vividly recall a breakthrough moment with a client during a culture analysis. They discovered that the stories they kept on sharing and believing were built on outdated assumptions about success, which were now hindering them from moving forward.

You Are a Storyteller

When my wife and I founded Heart Management in 2017, we lacked a consulting background and had minimal connections in the HR or business circles of Sweden. My wife's experience involved reviving a Scandinavian manufacturing company in Ukraine, while I had been running a communications agency primarily focused on nonprofit clients. United by a shared passion for organizational culture, we aspired to change how leaders approached it, yet we faced the challenge of finding clients without any clear strategy.

We decided to share our insights by creating a comprehensive online resource, freely sharing everything we had learned about values and culture change. Over time, this resource was downloaded thousands of times.

When the pandemic hit in 2020, our work dried up, and we struggled to see how the company would survive, which was particularly terrifying since both of our incomes were tied to the business. We spent many mornings in tears and desperation. However, despite the dire circumstances, we doubled down on generosity, launched a podcast and free webinars, and let our participants set their own price when we launched our first online culture course that spring. This led to a radical turnaround and opened the door to some incredible client relationships.

Sharing with radical generosity, even when it got costly, has been a key to our success and is a core value at our company.

What I've just told you is a story. It includes tension, struggles, transformation, and ultimately success. Factually correct and in my perception true, but a story nonetheless. A story that has become a part of the narrative of our company and has helped shape our culture. Instead of sharing this story, I could have said that our marketing strategy has been focused on inbound marketing (attracting customers to one's business by creating useful content). It would also be factually true, and it would require less vulnerability. However, it wouldn't capture your imagination or communicate anything meaningful about our mission and values.

Marshall Ganz, a senior lecturer at Harvard University renowned for his expertise in community organizing and social movements, wrote,

"Narrative is not talking 'about' values; rather narrative embodies and communicates values. And it is through the shared experience of our values that we can engage with others, motivate one another to act, and find the courage to take risks, explore possibility and face the challenges we must face."[4]

It is in the stories we share that our values are brought to life.

I've asked many groups of team members to share stories of what it looks like when their organization lives its values. You can often see, based on their response, whether these values are merely posters on the wall or an actual part of the fabric of the culture and shared experiences of the organization. It is when our mission and values are shared through stories that they shape beliefs and assumptions and can lead to a change of behavior.

Whether you are aware of it or not, you are a storyteller. You are constantly sharing stories that will shape your culture and have the potential to either reinforce your values or contradict them.

When you bump into someone at the watercooler, when you wait for your team members to gather for a digital or physical meeting, when you're sharing an update on the intranet or meeting a team member in a one-to-one or team meeting, you have opportunities to share stories and promote your values. Associate professor Mark Mortensen at INSEAD, who's an expert on hybrid collaboration, told me in a 2022 interview, "Culture is shared and transmitted through shared experience, but you can't always be there. Stories are a way to share experiences over time and over distance."[5]

To cultivate cultural health and make our values mean something, we must intentionally and consistently share stories that embody our mission and values.

Avoiding the Dark Side of Storytelling

In the early 2000s, France Télécom's then-CEO Didier Lombard saw a need to fire thousands of employees to stay competitive in a rapidly changing telecom market. However, they didn't have the legal grounds to let people go, according to French labor laws. So they devised a different plan. In a training program for middle managers, they created a narrative that painted team members who didn't have the right skills as dinosaurs that needed to be extinct. In contrast, managers who were great at pressuring employees to leave "voluntarily" were celebrated as heroes.

The narrative created a mind-bending reality, putting fundamental values like respect and empathy out of play. Managers began to make life miserable for team members—for example, by moving a senior technician to customer service without providing training or transferring an employee with a sick parent to an office in another city where they would be unable to provide the needed care. And employees did leave. Professor Guido Palazzo, having researched the France Télécom case extensively, told me, in a 2021 interview, that while some left through the door, others left "through the window"[6] and decided to end their lives in despair.

In December 2019, as a result of a tragic suicide wave at the company, Lombard and six other defendants were found guilty of moral harassment.[7]

Stories can be powerful tools to embody and promote our mission and values, yet they can also lead to a toxic culture and drive unethical behavior, as we've seen in the example of France Télécom. When researching corporate scandals, it's clear that business executives, in many cases, framed industry regulators as the enemies who were trying to limit and destroy their business. This narrative caused team members to take shortcuts on quality or even break legal rules.

Stories can bring people together, but they can also be a potent method for manipulation. A destructive community, like the one I belonged to, wouldn't have ever been able to continue if it weren't for the stories we were fed about how our community, particularly our founder, was special and had an extraordinarily important mission—and that people who challenged that mission or leadership suffered adverse consequences and never fulfilled their true purpose.

As John Gottschall, an American literary scholar and author of *Story Paradox*, puts it, "As soon as you're telling a story, you're in an ethically fraught situation. Because you're trying to use a form of messaging that is not explicit."[8]

Since storytelling can bypass a person's defenses, we should be very thoughtful about the stories we tell and how we tell them. A great place to start is to reflect on our motives and ask ourselves:

- Why are we telling this story?
- Who or what interests does it serve?
- Who does it portray as heroes and villains, and what are the consequences?
- Are the facts true, or are we distorting the truth to fit with our message?

Change Your Stories to Change Your Culture

Two consulting company executives contacted me about a need to deal with toxic cultural elements that were increasingly having a negative impact on their ability to hire and retain new talent. When I asked them what had shaped these elements of their culture, they shared stories about work conferences early on in the company's history. The founders and team members got heavily intoxicated, and there were sexual innuendos and lines crossed. However, as I heard them retell these stories, I realized they didn't sound appalled. Instead, even if they probably wouldn't have admitted it, they shared the stories with an ill-disguised sense of awe, as if they saw the behavior as somewhat heroic or inspiring. I told them that unless they were willing to address, rethink, and reframe those stories, I didn't believe they would be able (or willing) to change their culture.

The late Austrian philosopher Ivan Illich wrote,

"Neither revolution nor reformation can ultimately change a society, rather you must tell a new powerful tale, one so persuasive that it sweeps away the old myths and becomes the preferred story, one so inclusive that it gathers all the bits of our past and our present into a coherent whole, one that even shines some light into our future so that we can take the next step . . . If you want to change a society, then you have to tell an alternative story."[9]

I have found these words to ring true when it comes to culture change.

Since culture is built upon deep-seated beliefs and assumptions (that might not be entirely accurate) about what has made us successful in the past, to change our culture, we must tell authentic stories that connect the past with our present and desired future, helping clarify:

1. where we're coming from,
2. where we are and why we can't stay, and
3. where we are going and why we should get there.

It's important not to bad-mouth the past or cast yourself as a savior. Instead, we should honor the past but be clear on why things have to change to responsibly steward our organization's legacy.

So what might that look like in your organization?

Perhaps the stories of success that have shaped your culture may have reinforced the assumption of individualism and internal competition, but now you see a critical need for increased collaboration. To change that story, you need to spend time thinking about why going at it alone might have worked in the past but isn't working anymore. You need to make a compelling case for what a different future of increased collaboration would look like and why it matters to your team members. And you need to get clear on how you will take active responsibility to be a part of the change. And finally, you need to intentionally share stories that can help people make both emotional and intellectual sense of that transition.

One of our clients, a large multinational company, did this brilliantly. As the start of a culture and leadership program, we wanted the CEO to give a message on why they were committed to developing more values-driven and responsible leaders. Too often, these kinds of messages can feel half-hearted and sound like the person is reading a script from the communications department. However, he began by discussing what responsible leadership meant to him personally and to the company. Then he vulnerably addressed how reckless leadership actions in the company's past had cost large sums of money and why he believed that no company could be long-term financially successful at the expense of other stakeholders. Finally, he called out conflicting priorities between short-term profit versus building long-term stakeholder trust and clarified how he wanted his leaders and team members to think about those decisions, emphasizing why that mattered to the future of the company and every employee. The message left no doubt that he meant what he said and that it was personal to him.

As we explored in Practice 2, the most powerful and believable change story you can tell is done by taking ownership, taking action, and becoming a part of the positive change. It's not about framing yourself as the hero.

> *For your team to believe in the change you are proposing, they need to see that you are invested and that you promote the values not just with words but through your example.*

I'll close with a quote from *The Secret of Culture Change*, coauthored by Professor Jay Barney:

"Authentic stories reveal to your employees something fundamental about who you are and what you want to accomplish. For this reason, authentic stories reassure your employees that your commitment to cultural change is real and unchangeable. They know that your efforts to change the culture are not a whim, or ego-driven, or a transitory commitment, but instead are a manifestation of who you are as a person. When they hear the authentic stories you have built, they are more likely to join with you to cocreate your organization's new culture. But when the stories you build are inauthentic, they can have exactly the opposite effect. Your employees can smell hypocrisy miles away."[10]

Five Keys to Sharing Stories That Embody Mission and Values

We've discussed how stories shape culture and why all leaders are storytellers. Here are five keys to telling stories that embody your mission and values.

1 Reflect on the narratives that have shaped the culture in your team or organization.

The beliefs and narratives about your organization and its stakeholders will greatly influence your culture. Here are some questions to help you reflect on those beliefs and narratives and how they might hinder or enable your organization to deliver on its mission, build a thriving workplace, and have a responsible impact.

- What stories have shaped the culture in your organization?
- What values do they promote?
- What beliefs and assumptions have those stories created about your organization, its people, leadership, clients, and other important stakeholders?
- Are those stories aligned with or in conflict with your mission, strategy, values, and desired culture?

2 Identify relevant stories.

Here are some examples of stories that can be powerful vessels to communicate your mission and values:

- Historical narratives about the founding of your organization

- Examples of how you overcame some of your greatest challenges
- Examples of how you made decisions that were costly at the time because of values you didn't want to compromise
- Examples of your mission and values in action through team members' behaviors and initiatives
- Success stories from partners, clients, or other stakeholders who were helped by your services or products

---

You can also use questions to identify stories, such as:

- What has it looked like when your organization lived its mission and values in the past?
- What was the situation?
- Who were involved?
- What was the tension?
- Why did the values become important?

---

3 **Review avenues to share stories.**

All of us have different avenues to share stories. For example:

- Daily informal interactions with team members and peers
- Internal meetings
- A regular email update to our team or organization
- Posts on the intranet or other internal communication channels
- Meetings with clients or other important stakeholders

- External communication and marketing on social media or other platforms

Aim to be strategic about using the avenues you have at your disposal. For example, an executive team maintaining a biweekly internal blog or newsletter might decide that every edition should include a relevant story that embody their mission and values. Or a manager might decide to begin regular team meetings with a short story of a satisfied client.

4 Be sincere and authentic.

I've regularly encountered leaders writing glowing reviews about their amazing workplace, only to later seek our assistance in dealing with serious workplace issues. It's not that we should be flawless before we communicate good things; however, we should reflect on whether our team members feel like our external messaging is sincere. Otherwise, it may lead to frustration and resentment, stemming from a perceived sense of hypocrisy.

The same is true about how we communicate internally. While painting a vision for a great future is essential, avoid hyperbole and communication that might feel disconnected from people's reality. In my coaching experience with organizations undergoing crises, I've witnessed situations where leadership consistently communicated a cheerful message, despite their team members being well aware of the profound challenges at hand. Rather than providing genuine encouragement, it appeared tone deaf and insincere.

Don't be afraid to share stories that communicate both the successes and the challenges you're facing. As we explored in Practice 1, being vulnerable can build authenticity and trust with your team members.

5   Don't undermine the message.

A critical challenge in driving change is when executives and managers fail to communicate a unified message. Management Professor Henry Mintzberg provides a poignant metaphor: "Organizations don't have tops and bottoms . . . What organizations really have are the *outer* people, connected to the world, and the *inner* ones, disconnected from it, as well as many so-called *middle* managers, who are desperately trying to connect the inner and outer people to each other."[11]

If you are a senior executive, you need to ensure that you've solicited feedback and that the messages and stories you share about—for example, an important change initiative—are established with leaders throughout the organization and relevant to the realities of employees, as we discussed in Habit 3.

As middle managers and frontline leaders, you need to internalize the message, help make it relevant and applicable to your team members, and avoid communicating a conflicting story. Remember that you are representing the organization and its leadership. If you see issues with the decisions or narrative, speak up to superiors. However, avoid undermining their decisions in front of your team members. While it might not seem like a big deal, it creates confusion and a lack of clarity that will have negative consequences.

Finally, if you forget everything else, remember
that you are a storyteller, and the stories you
tell, especially through the example you set,
will have an immense impact on your culture.

Great leaders are great storytellers, and we can all get better with practice!

Reflection

- Which stories have played a crucial role in shaping your workplace culture?
- How can you more intentionally convey stories that authentically embody your mission and values?
- What avenues are available to you for sharing these stories?

Action

- Commit to implementing one specific change to more effectively share stories that embody mission and values. Consider the changes and challenges you observe over time.

The Practice at a Glance

The stories we share can authentically embody our mission, reinforce our values, and strengthen our culture or be ineffective and even become instruments of manipulation. To improve our cultural health, we need to embrace the role of storytellers, lead by example, rethink the stories we tell, and consider the methods we employ to tell them.

KEY QUOTE

" *Whether you are aware of it or not, you are a storyteller. You are constantly sharing stories that will shape your culture and have the potential to either reinforce your values or contradict them.* "

Further Resources

Books:

- *Creating Signature Stories: Strategic Messaging That Energizes, Persuades, and Inspires* by David Aaker
- *The Secret of Culture Change: How to Build Authentic Stories That Transform Your Organization* by Jay B. Barney, Manoel Amorim, and Carlos Júlio
- *The Story of Paradox: How Our Love of Storytelling Builds Societies and Tears them Down* by Jonathan Gottschall

Podcasts:

- "Avoiding Ethical Tunnel Vision"—my interview with Guido Palazzo on the *Leading Transformational Change* podcast
- "The 4Cs of Healthy and Adaptive Culture"—my interview with Jennifer Chatman on the *Leading Transformational Change* podcast
- "How Taking Ownership and Action Will Transform Your Culture"—my interview with Jay Barney on the *Leading Transformational Change* podcast

VISIT **YOUCANCULTURE.COM**
FOR MORE RESOURCES.

18

Practice 11:
Design Culture-Building Rituals

When Jungkiu Choi assumed the role of head of consumer banking at Standard Chartered Bank in China, he was told he needed to behave like an emperor—to reinforce the hierarchy, "keep the distance and retain mystique."[1]

An integral part of his new responsibilities involved annual visits to all bank branches. Traditionally, predecessors would announce their arrival two months in advance, prompting a flurry of activity among employees to spruce up the branch—"cleaning and painting the public areas and making all the filing systems neat."[2] As Choi would say, "The king always smells fresh paint." Unsurprisingly, most employees dreaded the visits.

Choi, however, felt like this was a pointless exercise since he wouldn't get an accurate picture of the reality of the branches or any genuine understanding of their needs or concerns. Therefore, he decided to reassess the ritual. Instead of giving a two-month notice, he decided to show up unannounced. Accompanied by his fellow executives, they would arrive early to prepare and serve breakfast to employees. After the meal, he would invite them to a "morning huddle," where Choi inquired about their problems and concerns, seeking ways to improve customer service. Team members sparked ideas such as adjusting the opening hours of a branch located in a shopping center to match the shopping center's, a change that significantly improved performance.

Over two years, Choi's branches witnessed a transformation from the highest to the lowest employee turnover and from the lowest to the highest customer service ratings among all banks.

Dan Cable, professor of organizational behavior at London Business School, tells the story of Jungkiu Choi's leadership in his book *Alive at Work*. Cable found that by rethinking the ritual, Choi *decreased distance* and built trust. Cable told me, in a 2022 interview, that "by listening to people's ideas, Choi unlocked potential, and that unlocked potential made a massive difference."[3]

To integrate critical habits and strengthen cultural health, we must develop culture-building rituals.

In Choi's case, rethinking both the ritual's design and content communicated to team members that their voices mattered. It repositioned Choi from being seen as an emperor to a servant leader. It created a radically new narrative about what the organization valued.

In our extensive experience working with various organizations, regardless of size, we've observed that you can't achieve lasting culture change, integrate values or sustain cultural health without assessing and redesigning your rituals.

Every Organization Has Its Rituals

How do you start or end your day? You probably have a few rituals that you hold tightly to. And chances are that the quality of your physical health, emotional and spiritual well-being, work effectiveness, and personal and work relationships are intimately tied to those rituals. John and Julie Gottman, two world-renowned clinical psychologists, are responsible for the most extensive study ever done on marital stability. Their research found that relational rituals are key to creating shared meaning and strengthening the bond in relationships.

John Gottman suggested that rituals such as (1) parting (learning "one thing that is happening in your partner's life that day before saying goodbye in the morning"), (2) reunion (to "share a hug and a kiss" when you meet again), (3) appreciation and admiration (to write down something you admire about your partner daily), (4) weekly date nights focused on romance, and (5) state of the union meetings to bring up fears and concerns are key to relationship quality and lasting relationships.[4] John Gottman wrote,

> "Every moment you're together, and even when you're not, you have an opportunity to honor all that is sacred in your relationship—however you define it."[5]

In the midst of some of the busiest periods while writing this book, I temporarily set aside several of my morning rituals. To find additional time for writing, I started waking up at four-thirty, heading to the office to write until returning home to prepare the kids for preschool by seven o'clock. As a morning person, rising at four-thirty posed no significant challenge. However, it was the neglect of other rituals that gradually took a toll. I missed the opportunity to kiss my wife, hug my kids, and engage in play with them as soon as they woke up, adversely affecting our relationships. Struggling to maintain my exercise routine also had an impact on my health. I failed to intentionally set aside time for practices vital to my emotional and spiritual well-being. While this approach might be sustainable for a short period, the abandonment of crucial rituals eventually led to personal and relational stress.

Just as rituals are vital to building personal or communal relationships, they play a critical role in shaping and upholding workplace culture. Every organization and team has rituals, routines, and actions that reinforce the organization's cultural beliefs, values, and identity, fostering a sense of cohesion and shared experience among its members. Professor Edgar Schein wrote that "culture implies that rituals, values, and behaviors are tied together into a coherent whole."[6]

> *Rituals communicate what we find significant and even sacred. They imbue meaning even into the mundane parts of everyday life. They connect us through shared experiences and give rise to collective memories and stories.*

If we are careful and intentional about our rituals, they can become powerful culture-building tools to communicate and integrate our mission and, most importantly, values.

Rituals of Connections

For several years, I led a remote team spanning two countries and four cities. Our work and collaboration primarily occurred through digital channels, but approximately twice a year, we gathered for a week to work from the same location. While our days were dedicated to work, we punctuated them with breaks to cook together, dine at a restaurant, or embark on long walks to explore the host city. These shared meals and experiences evolved into rituals of connection. Upon returning home, we would exchange experiences and stories, fostering reflection. These shared moments breathed life into our digital rituals, such as our Monday morning meetings, and the trust forged during these gatherings proved instrumental in enhancing collaboration during challenging times.

An illuminating study on firefighters and collaboration, by three researchers at Cornell University, found that the groups of firefighters who were most devoted to the ritual of making and sharing meals at the firehouse performed better than those who weren't.[7] Deb Mashek, a renowned collaboration researcher and social psychologist, found that our ability to collaborate effectively builds upon two factors: the level of relationship quality, that we trust each other and have a genuine sense of connection, and the level of interdependence, meaning "each person's outcomes are influenced by the other's behavior."[8] Mashek told me in a 2023 interview, "Every interaction is an opportunity to improve or degrade trust."[9]

Given that trusting relationships are essential for cultural health and collaboration, it's crucial to be highly intentional about the content and design of our rituals to ensure they cultivate trust and connection.

However, they don't have to be complicated and complex. Consider the simple ritual of acknowledging and greeting people when you arrive at work or digitally checking in with each other. Though seemingly small, I've heard numerous individuals express how these simple gestures significantly impact their experience of the work environment.

Examples of Culture-Building Rituals

Let's look at three impactful examples of culture-building rituals:

1. Rituals for commemoration

In August 2008, Maple Leaf Foods, a Canadian food production company, faced a listeria outbreak resulting in a tragic loss of twenty-three lives. Michael McCain, the company's then CEO quickly took responsibility and released a public apology. Most companies would have decided to leave what happened behind, to avoid dwelling on the negative. However, fourteen years later, the Maple Leaf Foods executive team still marks an annual commemoration ritual. McCain says they are "committed to never forget."[10]

One of our clients established a ritual, presenting an annual employee award in memory of a deceased colleague who epitomized the organization's values and spirit. This became a powerful ritual for connection and reflection on the company's values.

2. Rituals to spark ideas and innovation

At the Dutch retail giant C&A, CEO Giny Boer wanted to shift the culture to be less hierarchical and to encourage speaking up about problems, concerns, ideas, and failures. To facilitate the culture change, she instituted new rituals, such as a monthly "Let's

Connect" session, where people can sign up to pose questions to her or her chief people officer, and a twice monthly "Failure Friday," where three staff members share failures in an open and safe environment.[11]

3. Rituals to foster integration

One of our clients had merged with a similar but smaller company and wanted to strengthen collaboration and cohesiveness between the parts. One challenge was that the smaller company felt neglected and undervalued. The CEO decided that instead of having all the executive team meetings at the offices of the larger company, they would have every other meeting at the smaller company's offices. This communicated to the entire company that each part mattered, allowing the executive team to meet more team members and build trusting relationships. By rethinking the location of their meetings, they improved their cultural health.

REFLECTION

Consider the rituals in your workplace. Rituals of celebration like how you celebrate a sale, the launch of a project, or perhaps someone's birthday. Rituals of connection, like whether you have regular times to connect and check in with each other, for example, over coffee, a shared meal, or a set time for connection in a digital forum.

> What do these rituals communicate about your mission and values? How may they need to be redesigned? What might be missing?

There are countless things we can do to design and redesign rituals that help cultivate cultural health and communicate our values. However, we will now focus on how we can integrate conversations of culture and values into ubiquitous rituals that significantly influence our organizational culture—our routine meetings.

As Priya Parker, an expert on gathering, wrote in *The Art of Gathering*, "Gathering—the conscious bringing together of people for a reason—shapes the way we think, feel, and make sense of our world."[12]

A Ritual of Reflecting on Values

In Practice 1, I encouraged you to establish a ritual for regular personal reflection on your values and leadership—daily or at least a few times a week. Now, it's time to extend this practice to the team level.

At Heart Management we have initiated a dedicated thirty-minute meeting called Reflective. In this session, we reflect on our values, examining how our actions have aligned with them over the past weeks, and identify situations where we faced challenges or deviated from our values. It's seldom that we don't have valuable and instructive conversations with relevant examples of learnings and struggles. Sometimes, they lead to critical shifts in our culture and strategy, while at other times, they help address minor concerns and relational issues that, if ignored, could escalate into major problems. The consistent takeaway, however, is that they are always beneficial.

I recommend implementing a similar ritual within your team. Many of our clients integrate these conversations into their regular team meeting agenda, whether on a weekly, biweekly, or monthly basis. I believe these conversations should take place at every level, including in the executive team. You might think you don't have time, but I'm confident having these conversations regularly will save you time otherwise spent on numerous cultural challenges and unaddressed concerns that could derail you.

Suggested Agenda

Take a moment to read through your mission, values, and critical behaviors. Then ask the following questions (give time for the participants to reflect for a minute individually first or give them even more time to write down their thoughts, as we discussed in Practice 8):

- Where have we acted in line with our mission and values this last week/month (e.g., taken the initiative to innovate, delivered excellent customer service, contributed to collaboration, or acted ethically)?
- Where have we struggled or faced values dilemmas or concerns?
- If there is time: What will we be doing differently going forward?
- Discuss your responses together.

It might take a few times to get the conversation going. You might also find yourself with a large number of issues surfacing that you now need to find ways to address. Remember, practice makes perfect, and the more consistently you engage in this ritual, the more at ease you'll become with it.

In my experience, genuine and honest questions about values and culture resonate with everyone, whether your team consists of lawyers or blue-collar workers at a manufacturing site.

I also suggest the following questions specifically for management teams (they may need to take place in a separate meeting).

- What decisions are we considering that have a values/ethical implication that we need to pay extra attention to?
- What positive initiatives and behaviors have we noticed that we should learn from, support, and communicate further?
- What tensions or dilemmas have we noticed that we need to address?

When management teams have these conversations, they can ensure that critical issues and dilemmas are appropriately handled at the relevant level.

A Ritual of Culture-Building 1:1 Meetings

In cultivating trust and connection through rituals, few are as crucial as regular 1:1 meetings with your direct reports.

Effective 1:1 meetings build trust, help your team members overcome hurdles and grow, and create opportunities to solicit feedback.

Unless we operate within a very small team with constant

communication, the opportunity for specific, scheduled one-on-one time with one's manager is often vital. I've encountered highly experienced leaders in senior positions who face challenges because their leaders, often the CEO, are unwilling to invest time in regular 1:1 meetings.

Professor Steven Rogelberg, renowned as the world's leading expert on meetings and the author of *Glad We Met*, conducted extensive research on 1:1 meetings. His findings reveal a direct correlation not only to employees thriving but also to managerial success, given that a manager's performance is often intricately tied to the team's success.[13] Rogelberg told me, in a 2023 interview, that 1:1s are where "leadership comes alive and where your employees see your values in action."[14] It's an opportunity to show that our organization genuinely values the success of our team members.

Here are ten helpful tips for culture-building 1:1s, based on Rogelberg's recommendations:

1. Focus on the team member. Remember that these meetings are about your team members and their growth, not just your managerial agenda.
2. Avoid canceling meetings as it sends the message that the employee is low on your priority list. If rescheduling is necessary, opt for an earlier date rather than a later one.
3. Tie your conversations to organizational and personal values, reinforcing the connection between individual goals and the broader mission.

4. Aim for twenty to thirty minutes weekly or forty-five to sixty minutes every other week. Adjust the duration based on the number of direct reports you manage.

5. Collaboratively create an agenda with your team members, encouraging them to contribute points for discussion. Alternatively, use a set of relevant and helpful questions.

6. Strive to listen more than you speak, creating an environment where your team members feel heard and valued.

7. Actively seek feedback from your team members, fostering a culture of openness and continuous improvement. Ask questions like, "What feedback do you have for me?"

8. Use these meetings as an opportunity to collaboratively solve problems and address challenges your team members may face.

9. Acknowledge and express gratitude for your team member's contributions, reinforcing their value within the organization.

10. Make notes during the meeting and follow up on action items or discussions in subsequent sessions, demonstrating your commitment to progress.

I'll end with something I wrote at the beginning of this practice. If we are careful and intentional about our rituals, they can become powerful culture-building tools to communicate and integrate our mission and most important values and help sustain cultural health.

You Can Culture   Month 11

Reflection

- Do you currently have established rituals for consistent and robust reflection with your team on culture and values?
- How well do these rituals serve their purpose in your organization?
- What adjustments can be made to ensure your rituals create connection, build trust, and help sustain cultural health?

Action

- Commit to incorporating a ritual that facilitates robust conversations about your values, culture, and decisions. Consider the changes and challenges you observe over time.
- If you already have the above ritual in place, pledge to make one adjustment to another ritual that could contribute to fostering connection and strengthening your culture.

The Practice at a Glance

Every team engages in rituals where relationships are built, stories are told, priorities are set, and decisions are made. These rituals greatly impact the health of our teams and the quality of our professional relationships. To sustain cultural health, we must design culture-building rituals that foster connection and ongoing conversations about our mission, values, and behaviors.

" *Rituals communicate what we find significant and even sacred. They imbue meaning even into the mundane parts of everyday life. They connect us through shared experiences and give rise to collective memories and stories.* "

Further Resources

Books:

- *Glad We Met: The Art and Science of 1:1 Meetings* by Steven G. Rogelberg
- *Alive at Work: The Neuroscience of Helping Your People Love What They Do* by Daniel M. Cable
- *Collabor(h)ate: How to Build Incredible Collaborative Relationships at Work* by Deb Mashek

Podcasts:

- "Why One-on-One Meetings Are Vital for Cultural Health and How to Make Them Better"—my interview with Steven G. Rogelberg on the *Leading Transformational Change* podcast
- "Connecting People with Purpose"—my interview with Dan Cable on the *Leading Transformational Change* podcast
- "Building a Healthy Culture in a Hybrid World"—my interview with Mark Mortensen on the *Leading Transformational Change* podcast
- "Why Collaboration Sucks and What To Do about It"—my interview with Deb Mashek on the *Leading Transformational Change* podcast

VISIT **YOUCANCULTURE.COM**
FOR MORE RESOURCES.

19

Practice 12:
Rethink Incentives and Processes for Cultural Health

All companies in our industry have these problems. This is just how it's done in our line of work. It's impossible to change that in this type of environment.

I've often heard leaders try to excuse their cultural challenges with sentiments like these. While industry-specific dynamics might need to be addressed, it's interesting to look at organizations that have managed to build a different culture and get radically different results, even though others might claim it's impossible.

One outlier in an industry known for subpar customer service and high employee turnover is the Atlanta-based fast-food chain Chick-fil-A. While you could argue whether their chicken sandwich, first served in 1964, is better or worse than their competitors' equivalents (there is a heated debate about that online), it's clearly not the product that is the key to their outstanding success.

The company has the highest customer satisfaction scores year after year[1] and the highest revenue per restaurant by far, about 70 percent higher than McDonald's, even though they're famously closed on Sundays. You'll notice the difference when ordering at one of their thousands of restaurants. Instead of a half-hearted "You're welcome," Chick-fil-A team members reply, "It's my pleasure," often with a smile.

There are countless stories of team members going above and beyond to serve their clients, such as changing a flat tire for a ninety-six-year-old customer or bringing free food to motorists stranded in a snowstorm in Alabama.[2] You won't be surprised to know that one of Chick-fil-A's core values is "We're here to serve." One of the world's largest studies on organizational culture, done by researchers at MIT, identified Chick-fil-A as a culture champion that walks the walk when it comes to collaboration and customer orientation.[3]

While it's clear Chick-fil-A has been intentional about integrating many of the culture-building practices I've highlighted so far in this book, they've also worked hard on setting processes and incentives that would support cultural health as they grew. One example is how they select new restaurant operators.

Chick-fil-A receives about sixty thousand franchisee applications, but only opens seventy-five to eighty stores annually. While other major fast-food chains like McDonald's[4] have franchise fees of about $45,000 and require that you have at least $500,000 in liquid assets,[5] Chick-fil-A has a franchise fee of only $10,000 and no liquid asset requirements. While many other chains allow their franchisees to operate multiple locations, Chick-fil-A rarely does.

The reason is that Chick-fil-A wants to attract restaurant operators who care deeply about serving their local community and want to be personally involved with developing leaders and providing excellent customer service, not people who see their franchise as a mere financial investment.

In a similar way, they are very particular about who they recruit to their restaurants or Support Center (as their corporate office is called). As vice president of corporate talent at Chick-fil-A, Dee Ann Turner, author of *Bet on Talent*, was instrumental in putting hiring processes in place to build and support a culture of service—for example, being rigorous about behavioral interview questions. During her tenure, the company became known for selecting some of the best talent in the hospitality business, maintaining a 95 percent retention rate for corporate staff and franchisees. In 2020, Chick-fil-A was named one of the top one hundred best places to work by Glassdoor.[6]

Turner told me, in a 2018 interview, that early in the company's history, Chick-fil-A realized they weren't in the chicken business but in the people business,[7] believing that,

> "If you select the right person again and again, the collection of the character, competency and chemistry of those people would develop and strengthen the culture over time."[8]

Chick-fil-A built those beliefs and values into its franchisee approval and hiring processes, and it helped them sustain a culture of collaboration and excellent customer service. They became different by design.

However, as we'll soon see, organizations often struggle with a misalignment between stated values and the signals their processes and incentives send.

The Danger of Misaligned Incentives

Richard Bistrong had an admirable career. After finishing his master's degree at the University of Virginia, he enrolled in a PhD program in foreign affairs and was offered a White House Fellowship in the Reagan administration. However, he decided to leave the world of academia to enter commercial sales within the law enforcement and defense field. After many successful years as a sales leader focusing on the US market, selling lifesaving equipment including armored vehicles and armored vests to US law enforcement and military agencies, he was offered the job of vice president of international sales to help the company expand into emerging markets.[9]

Before commencing his role, he was asked to sign the US Foreign Corrupt Practices Act (FCPA) paperwork and explicitly informed that these laws and principles should guide his behavior. He was assigned aggressive sales targets and lucrative bonus incentives—demonstrating remarkable success in his new position, traveling extensively, and securing new business throughout the globe.

The first time he confronted corruption, he was meeting with a third-party distributor (agent) in South America. The agent told him that they were sure to win a large upcoming public sector procurement but he had paid "tolls." While Bistrong had never heard the expression before in such a context, he understood that the distributor was paying some kind of bribe to win the contract. He nodded his head at this new information. This was the first time he violated the FCPA; however, it would not be the last.

Bistrong told me, in a 2020 interview, that there is "truly such a thing as a slippery slope."[10]

He gradually moved from turning a blind eye to bribery to becoming personally involved. While he knew that what he was doing was wrong and illegal, he deceived himself first. Bistrong rationalized it by telling himself that everyone else was doing it, that it didn't hurt anyone, and he began to question whether the company cared most about achieving their aggressive sales targets or following the law (because he felt he couldn't do both). He shared with me that, due to no one's fault but his own, he felt that he was in the middle of competing corporate objectives between the pressure to succeed and the pressure to comply, but he didn't ask for help or support to unpack that tension.

However, it would all come to an end. After being targeted by the US Department of Justice, he assisted the US and UK governments undercover as part of a cooperation agreement. In 2012, he began serving fourteen-and-a-half months in prison.

Today, Bistrong speaks and advises leaders worldwide on ethics and compliance challenges based on his personal experiences. He is the first to state that he bears full responsibility for the actions that landed him in prison. However, he's also found that, too often, organizations don't talk openly about the risks and dilemmas of, for example, doing business in high-risk and volatile markets. Instead, they too often ask their team members to sign codes of conduct and leave them alone to navigate the tension between very aggressive sales goals with lucrative financial incentives and company values with compliance "guardrails."

How to Avoid Mixed Signals

Throughout this book, I've made the case that culture is shaped by signals communicating what behaviors are encouraged and rewarded, disregarded, or not accepted. Our values should help us clarify those signals. However, too often, there's some mismatch between the values we claim and the signals we send. We might say we want innovation, but we punish failure. We discuss the importance of long-term goals but reward short-term results. We say we trust our team members but have control systems in place that build on distrust. We encourage teamwork but only incentivize individual performance.

Or as in the case of Bistrong, we say we want people to abide by the law, but then we have aggressive sales goals in unstable markets, with nearly unlimited bonus opportunities.

When we say we value one thing and then incentivize or create processes that encourage conflicting behavior, we begin to send mixed signals. And the result is that we often get the behavior we incentivize, not the behavior we claim we want.

As you've been working through the eleven practices we've covered so far, you've begun to get humble and admit that you and your organization are vulnerable and should not take cultural health for granted. You've made your values clear and begun to celebrate the right behavior and not accept behavior that is destructive to your culture. You've begun to solicit feedback and listen more intently to dilemmas and concerns. And you've begun to take ownership and become even more intentional about leading by example.

However, I'm sure that along the way, a certain sense of dissonance has come up in your mind or in conversations with your team members. You've realized, for example, that your organization isn't as intentional about its processes as Dee Ann Turner was with the recruitment process in the example of Chick-fil-A. Or perhaps you've realized that there are incentives in place that are misaligned with your values, and your team members are facing constant tensions between competing values that aren't adequately addressed.

Almost every client we've worked with has at some point realized that to be successful and sustain cultural health, they need to redesign and set processes and incentives that promote the right behavior and support their cultural health.

Processes owned by HR—such as recruitment and retention, onboarding and off-boarding, performance management, compensation and benefits, and learning and development—are often high on the list. However, there are many others that are equally vital. For example, strategic planning, budget allocation, corporate governance, supply chain management, and technology integration all impact priorities, decisions, and ultimately culture.

For a tech company client, integrating their mission and values meant defining principles that would guide their design process. A client in the public health care sector needed to ensure their processes enabled better collaboration in the patient care journey.

REFLECTION

I want to encourage you to reflect on the following questions:

- What processes or incentives have you found to be helping or hindering your ability to deliver on your mission, build a thriving workplace, and have responsible impact?
- What processes or incentive structures do you own, have the ability to influence directly, or participate in?
- What can you do, or who could you talk to, to help bring change?

Now, I understand that depending on your role within your organization, you might have ownership of several key processes, or you might not have any influence over them at all. However, even the way you participate in processes matters.

Regular Cultural Health Assessments

Most organizations have some form of regular employee engagement survey process. However, as I pointed out in chapter 1, culture is more than employee engagement. Our team has even been called in to help organizations with impressive results on their employee engagement surveys that still ended up in crises because of cultural health issues and a toxic workplace.

Let's imagine that a family struggling with unhealthy dynamics visits a family therapist. The therapist wouldn't (hopefully) try to benchmark the family against all other families in the country but begin to observe and assess behavioral patterns, assumptions, and roles. The same should be true of our efforts to assess our cultural health.

Professor Edgar Schein wrote that "culture assessment may require both a quantitative assessment (valid questionnaires in statistically significant quantities) and conversational assessment with individuals and groups inside the organization to provide feedback and to make sense of the data."[11] He describes that as "combining the diagnostic and/or the dialogic approach."[12]

Knowing that 25 percent of your organization feels somewhat unsafe speaking up about concerns would give you an indication of the problem. However, to understand why, you need to hear the stories and perspectives of your team members.

Over the years we've helped many organizations assess their culture and found that by asking open-ended questions through workshops, surveys, and interviews in combination with quantitative questions, you get a much better understanding of the beliefs, assumptions, and values that guide behavioral patterns within the organization.

Some of the things we want to understand are as follows:

- What behaviors are believed to be encouraged and rewarded?
- How are positive behaviors rewarded?
- What bad behaviors are tolerated?
- How are bad behaviors dealt with?
- Do people feel safe speaking up about concerns?
- Where do team members see a disconnect between values and actions?
- When did team members see the organization make a costly decision to uphold its values and principles?

I would recommend that you find a way to regularly make a deeper assessment of your cultural health and that you combine that with adding questions to employee engagement surveys that can help you better measure progress over time.

Rethinking and Redesigning Incentives and Processes

Do you enjoy performance reviews? I've heard many people, both managers and team members, find performance reviews unfair, irrelevant, and even dehumanizing. Rather than looking forward to conversations with their manager about their job performance, many team members dread those moments and feel like their manager has little understanding of their contribution.

Ron Carucci, author of *To Be Honest* who's studied the impact of performance reviews, told me in a 2021 interview, "The processes that should be the most dignifying and the most honoring have become the most dehumanizing and demeaning."[13] A 2017 study by Gallup found that "only two in ten employees strongly agree that their performance is managed in a way that motivates them to do outstanding work."[14] According to a Corporate Executive Board survey of thirteen thousand employees worldwide, "66 percent of employees say the performance review process interferes with their productivity, and 65 percent say it isn't even relevant to their jobs."[15]

The debates around how to fix performance reviews have gone on for years, and different organizations have chosen different approaches to rectify them. However, if a process isn't working, it will not help to merely add a list of our values and behaviors. We might need to reimagine it.

I've worked with organizations that needed to implement more robust governance and compliance processes to help ensure checks and balances and create safe avenues for speaking up. I've worked with other organizations that needed to eliminate processes and measurements that only added undue burdens on their employees.

Our processes and incentives should enable our team members to do their best work, not hinder them. They should build trust with our people, not undermine it. They should encourage people to act in line with our values, not push them to break them.

Questions to Rethink Your Processes and Incentives

To improve our processes and ensure they support our cultural health, we need to continually assess them, asking questions like:

- What is the purpose and objective of this process?
- Is it fulfilling that objective?
- What does the way this process is designed and implemented communicate that our organization values?
- Is the process building or undermining trust with our team members, clients, or relevant stakeholders?
- Do we regularly survey whether people influenced by the process find it helpful or hindering?

In the same way, we need to be intentional about the incentives we use. Professor Uri Gneezy, author of *Mixed Signals* and an expert on incentives, told me in a 2023 interview that incentives often don't work exactly as we assume, and that's why we have to design and redesign them to ensure that we achieve the desired outcomes while keeping our eyes open to possible unintended consequences.[16]

Here are some things to consider when designing incentives, with inspiration from Gneezy:

- Be clear on what positive behaviors you want to promote and reinforce through your incentives.
- Be aware of unintended consequences. Adding new incentives might diminish intrinsic motivation or lead to unethical behavior.
- Be transparent with your incentives. Tell team members the rationale behind what you are trying to accomplish and what values you aim to promote.
- Try to find a balance between short-term results and long-term sustainability. While short-term incentives may drive immediate performance, ensure they don't undermine long-term health.
- Assess incentives regularly and invite input from fellow leaders or team members who can tell you what is working and what possible unintended consequences they might be experiencing.

Ultimately, we must ensure that every signal sent through our incentives and processes reinforces positive behaviors in line with our mission, strategy, and most important values.

Don't try to fix it all at once, but start somewhere and keep working your way through and assessing the change. It will be well worth the work as you set processes that can sustain cultural health.

You Can Culture   Month 12

Reflection

- What processes and incentives could risk encouraging behavior that conflict with your mission and values?
- How could you help ensure that your organization's most critical incentives and processes help sustain cultural health?
- What could your organization do to keep assessing cultural health going forward?

Action

- Commit to making some contribution to adjust or utilize incentives or processes in a way that would better support cultural health. If you can't directly impact the processes or incentives in place, start raising your concerns and offering suggestions to people in charge.

The Practice at a Glance

Too often, there's a dissonance between the values we claim and the signals we send through our incentives and processes. To get integrity, we must ensure that our incentives and processes don't foster dangerous tensions but instead help sustain cultural health over time. It requires committed effort and continuous adjustments.

" *We must ensure that every signal sent through our incentives and processes reinforces positive behaviors in line with our mission, strategy, and, most important values.* "

Further Resources

Books:

- *Mixed Signals: How Incentives Really Work* by Uri Gneezy
- *To Be Honest: Lead with the Power of Truth, Justice, and Purpose* by Ron Carucci

Podcasts:

- "Avoiding Mixed Signals—How to Align Incentives with Values"—my interview with Uri Gneezy on the *Leading Transformational Change* podcast
- "Leading at the Ethics Edge"—my interview with Susan Liautaud on the *Leading Transformational Change* podcast
- "Rehumanizing Organizations through Truth, Justice, and Purpose"—my interview with Ron Carucci on the *Leading Transformational Change* podcast

VISIT **YOUCANCULTURE.COM**
FOR MORE RESOURCES.

Conclusion

"How did you go bankrupt?" Bill asked. "Two ways,"
Mike said. "Gradually and then suddenly."[1]

—Ernest Hemingway

I remember standing in front of the mirror and suddenly realizing that my body had gone through a transformation. The slouching posture I had become so accustomed to was replaced by an upright, confident stance. My chest was more pronounced, my gut had noticeably shrunk, and my biceps were toned and defined. The reflection showed someone fit, perhaps even strong—a stark contrast to the image I was used to.

I felt a transformation within me too. There was this newfound urge to train harder, to push myself to new limits. Healthy eating suddenly seemed not just desirable but essential. I could hardly believe it. And yet the transformation wasn't as sudden as it seemed. It was the culmination of consistent effort and a gradual journey over many months to a healthier, stronger self. It happened, to quote Hemingway, "gradually and then suddenly."

How could an organization that had seemed driven by a noble mission become so toxic?

How could I, who saw myself as an ethical and values-driven leader, become complicit in psychological abuse?

In the introduction, I posed the two questions that have haunted me for years and that I've desperately sought to understand. And the answer is that it happened gradually and then suddenly. Like the slow boiling of the proverbial frog. A long journey over an extended period of time, marked by subtle shifts in direction and numerous red flags that were dismissed, led to a destination I don't think any of us on the inside would have imagined—a place with lingering effects that continue to unfold.

Yet there's a silver lining. Just as leadership can insidiously devolve into toxicity and cultural health can deteriorate, the reverse is equally true.

Both your leadership and workplace culture can experience a positive change and even transformation. This change, too, often happens through a gradual process that can over time lead to a transformative shift.

You might not have personally noticed the signs of change along the way, but as you look back, you realize how far you've come and that the leader you are now is a radically different person than the leader you once were. I'm grateful to have had that experience in my own journey as a leader, husband, and father.

As you've gone on your journey through this book, you've been learning to do the following:

1. *Get humble*—embrace vulnerability, take ownership and action, and repair broken trust in order to avoid blindness and build and sustain trust and cultural health.

2. *Get clear*—clarify your most important values, celebrate the right behaviors, and deal with unhelpful or destructive behavior in order to build engagement and foster healthy behavioral patterns that enable mission success and a thriving workplace.
3. *Get listening*—solicit feedback, create conditions for brave conversations, and exercise voicing values in order to break the silence, avoid blindness, and get valuable feedback to improve your leadership, your team, and the organization at large.
4. *Get integrity*—share stories that promote your vision and values, design culture-building rituals, and set processes in order to ensure integrity and sustain cultural health over time.

As you've begun to reflect and act on these critical culture-building habits and practices, I'm confident that something has begun to shift. Whether you've noticed it or not, things are changing.

I remember a client who was so concerned they weren't seeing the needed change within their leadership and culture. However, sometime later their HR manager contacted me, overjoyed to share the radical change they'd seen evidenced in the three-year shift of their engagement survey. They kept doing the work and developing the habits and practices, and over time it led to significant results. I'm confident that you'll have similar experiences.

Habits Require Consistent Effort

Change is seldom a straight line, and there's often a messy middle. And as I've said repeatedly, the journey of integrating these habits and building cultural health is one that's never done. There will always be new challenges to tackle, always new situations to apply them to. And at times, I'm sure you'll realize you've lost sight of some practice in this book you had assumed you would never turn back on.

As I'm writing these sentences, I know I need to get back to healthier habits. Having spent months of early mornings finishing off this manuscript, I've walked back on some important habits and rituals. The same will be true in your leadership.

There will be times when you get so busy or distracted by other priorities. When that happens, don't be too hard on yourself. But remember that just like the health of your physical heart, your cultural health matters. And neglecting it will result in consequences over time.

So get back at it again.

Find your rhythm of personal reflection. Continue engaging in difficult conversations with your team. Keep striving to make more values-driven decisions. Keep being committed to recognizing and celebrating your team members' contributions. Keep making the tough decisions to deal with bad behavior, even when it's inconvenient.

As I said in the introduction, these critical culture-building habits aren't complex, but they are challenging. They will challenge your comfort, and you can't relegate them to someone else.

You have to, as a leader, take
ownership and be the change.

However, I'm 100 percent convinced that you can change your leadership and culture if you choose to keep at it and don't give up.

Taking the Next Step

Writing a book proved to be a much greater challenge than I initially anticipated. Through the ups and downs, I've often been tempted to give up. However, I haven't been able to let go because with every day and every interaction with leaders facing challenges, the message felt increasingly vital. I knew I had to write it (and my wife wouldn't forgive me if I didn't finish this book).

At the end of the day, my one desire and hope for this book was that it would help you grow into a values-driven leader, equipped to cultivate and sustain a thriving workplace and a culture that delivers. If it served this purpose for you, I want to encourage you to do two things:

1. Share your story with our team at youcanculture.com.
2. Share the book with a friend or colleague who you believe might need it.

Thank you for contributing to a world where organizations with a healthy culture become the norm and not the exception.

Your leadership, your team, your organization, and the world will be better because of it!

And never forget, *you can culture!*

Notes

Introduction

1   "Elie Wiesel Nobel Lecture," The Nobel Prize, December 11, 1986, https://www.nobelprize.org/prizes/peace/1986/wiesel/lecture/.

2   Donald Sull, Charles Sull, and Ben Zweig, "Toxic Culture Is Driving the Great Resignation," *MIT Sloan Management Review*, January 11, 2022, https://sloanreview.mit.edu/article/toxic-culture-is-driving-the-great-resignation/.

3   Ryan Pendell, "Employee Engagement Strategies: Fixing the World's $8.8 Trillion Problem," Gallup, September 11, 2023, https://www.gallup.com/workplace/393497/world-trillion-workplace-problem.aspx.

4   SHRM, "SHRM Reports Toxic Workplace Cultures Cost Billions," September 25, 2019, https://www.shrm.org/about/press-room/shrm-reports-toxic-workplace-cultures-cost-billions.

5   Deloitte Development LLC, "Cultural Issues in Mergers and Acquisitions," 2009, https://www2.deloitte.com/content/dam/Deloitte/us/Documents/mergers-acqisitions/us-ma-consulting-cultural-issues-in-ma-010710.pdf.

6   Harvard Law School Forum on Corporate Governance, "Trust Survey: Key Findings and Lessons for Business Executives," April 30, 2023, https://corpgov.law.harvard.edu/2023/04/30/trust-survey-key-findings-and-lessons-for-business-executives/.

7   Niki Goodridge, "Only 15% of Organizations Succeed in Transforming Their Cultures," The i4cp Productivity Blog, March 21, 2019, https://www.i4cp.com/press-releases/only-15-of-organizations-succeed-in-transforming-their-cultures.

8   Olivia Williams, "Is This the World's Fittest Pensioner?" *Daily Mail*, February 11, 2013, https://www.dailymail.co.uk/news/article-2277081/ The-worlds-fittest-pensioner-Charles-Eugster-entering-international-sports-competitions-year.html.

9   Matt Blake, "The Healthiest Old Person on the Planet Explains How to Stay in Shape," *Vice*, April 11, 2016, https://www.vice.com/en/article/nn9xzg/ charles-eugster-fittest-oap-on-planet.

Chapter 1

1   Edgar H. Schein and Peter A. Schein, *The Corporate Culture Survival Guide Third Edition* (John Wiley & Sons, 2019), chap 3, Kindle.

2   Boris Groysberg, Jeremiah Lee, Jesse Price, and J. Yo-Jud Cheng, "The Leader's Guide to Corporate Culture," *Harvard Business Review*, January–February 2018, https://hbr.org/2018/01/the-leaders-guide-to-corporate-culture.

3   Edgar H. Schein, *Organizational Culture and Leadership 5th Edition* (John Wiley & Sons, 2017), chap 2, Kindle.

4   Boris Groysberg, Jeremiah Lee, Jesse Price, and J. Yo-Jud Cheng, "The Leader's Guide to Corporate Culture." *Harvard Business Review*, January–February 2018, https://hbr.org/2018/01/the-leaders-guide-to-corporate-culture.

5   Siobhan McHale, *The Insider's Guide to Culture Change: Creating a Workplace That Delivers, Grows, and Adapts* (HarperCollins Leadership, 2020), chap 2, Kindle.

6   Tobias Sturesson, "027. Jennifer Chatman: The 4Cs of Healthy & Adaptive Culture," December 3, 2020, in *Leading Transformational Change*, https://open.spotify.com/episode/3iy5ZCskOX6ZZ3orETx3Oy?si=dd7f 9ceb78664204.

7   Tobias Sturesson, "031. Stan Slap: Why You Must Know Your Organization's Cultural Obsession," February 12, 2021, in *Leading Transformational Change*, https://open.spotify.com/episode/2DDFhZOgayE633GPpqADBx? si=580044c355c04133.

8   Carolyn Taylor, *Walking the Talk: Building a Culture for Success* (Random House, 2005), chap 5, Kindle.

9   "The Wrong Ways to Strengthen Culture," *Harvard Business Review*,
     July–August 2019, https://hbr.org/2019/07/the-wrong-ways-to-strengthen-
     culture.

Chapter 2

1   Aleksandr Solzhenitsyn, *The Gulag Archipelago: An Experiment in Literary
     Investigation The Gulag Archipelago* (YMCA-Press, 1973), 1918–1956.
2   "Ledare: Så här självrättfärdigt får inte en myndighet agera," *Dagens Nyheter*,
     August 3, 2020, https://www.dn.se/ledare/sa-har-sjalvrattfardigt-far-inte-en-
     myndighet-agera/.
3   Filip Yifter-Svensson, "Har en värdegrund något värde?" Sydsvenskan,
     Kultur, August 30, 2020, https://www.sydsvenskan.se/2020-08-30/har-en-
     vardegrund-nagot-varde.
4   Tobias Sturesson, "024. Michaela Ahlberg & Anna Romberg: Culture
     and Ethics in a Corruption Scandal," October 20, 2021, in *Leading
     Transformational Change*, https://open.spotify.com/episode/0n5DODZukI
     AbEOGHenqqAL?si=4fb0ccfe7ef645bc&nd=1&dlsi=4a3e681172834a42.
5   Tobias Sturesson, "026. Ann Tenbrunsel: Overcoming our Ethical
     Blindspots," November 12, 2020, in *Leading Transformational Change*,
     https://open.spotify.com/episode/5PWClXahuDxUooOVXg1yU5?si=3479
     1aa47ff6407f.&nd=1&dlsi=32ec9381640f4375.
6   Ann E. Tenbrunsel and David M. Messick, "Ethical Fading: The Role of Self-
     Deception in Unethical Behavior," *Social Justice Research* 17, no. 2 (January
     2004): 223–236. https://www.researchgate.net/publication/227229550_
     Ethical_Fading_The_Role_of_Self-Deception_in_Unethical_Behavior.
7   "Volkswagen's Emissions Evasion," Ethics Unwrapped - McCombs School
     of Business – The University of Texas at Austin, accessed February 2, 2024,
     https://ethicsunwrapped.utexas.edu/video/volkswagens-emissions-evasion.
8   Brett Beasley, "Keep Ethics from 'Fading' When You Face a Tough Decision,"
     Notre Dame Deloitte Center for Ethical Leadership, accessed February 2,
     2024, https://ethicalleadership.nd.edu/news/ethical-fading-dont-let-ethics-
     fade-from-view/.
9   Tobias Sturesson, "065. Ann E. Tenbrunsel: Are We as Ethical as We Think?"
     November 2022, in *Leading Transformational Change*, https://open.spotify.
     com/episode/6G7nOPCVCqpSstUlk7BEeB?si=46d7265419a34788&nd=1
     &dlsi=ee944b3c39734e9c.

Chapter 3

1   Will Durant, *The Story of Philosophy* (Dorling Kindersley Publishing, 1926).

2   James Clear, *Atomic Habits* (Random House, 2018), chap 1, Kindle.

3   Phillippa Lally, Cornelia H. M. van Jaarsveld, Henry W. W. Potts, and Jane Wardle, "How Are Habits Formed: Modeling Habit Formation in the Real World," *European Journal of Social Psychology* 40, no. 6 (October 2010), https://www.researchgate.net/publication/32898894_How_are_habits_formed_Modeling_habit_formation_in_the_real_world.

Habit 1

1   "Augustine of Hippo," Goodreads, accessed February 2, 2024, https://www.goodreads.com/quotes/119814-do-you-wish-to-rise-begin-by-descending-you-plan.

Chapter 5

1   Tobias Sturesson, "025. Lenny Wong: Uncovering a Culture of Dishonesty," November 2020, in *Leading Transformational Change*, https://open.spotify.com/episode/0DCTBO6TVIxdfNw7SZHbWI?si=7bd8b53c57ae4935&nd=1&dlsi=4a027e868bc34a89.

2   Leonard Wong and Stephen J. Gerras, *Lying to Ourselves: Dishonesty in the Army Profession* (US Army War College Press, 2015), 51.

3   Ray Pompon, "Living in an Assume Breach World," Help Net Security. August 24, 2017, https://www.helpnetsecurity.com/2017/08/24/assume-breach-world/.

4   Daniel Coyle, *The Culture Code: The Secrets of Highly Successful Groups* (Random House, 2018), chap 8, Kindle.

5   Adam Grant, *Think Again* (Ebury Publishing, 2021), chap 2, Kindle.

6   Brené Brown, *Daring Greatly* (Penguin Books, 2012), chap 2, Kindle.

Chapter 6

1   Greenpeace International, "In 2006, Greenpeace asked companies . . . " October 13, 2011, https://m.facebook.com/greenpeace.international/photos/a.165558403299/10150333286358300/?type=3.

2   Kelly April Tyrrell, "Study Shows Brazil's Soy Moratorium Still Needed to Preserve Amazon," *Science* 347, no. 6220 (January 23 2015): 377–378.

3   Tobias Sturesson, "041. Bob Langert: Collaborating with Your Toughest Critics," September 2021, in *Leading Transformational Change*, https://open.spotify.com/episode/3C06iNiVrPhtVmgd0ypGXu?si=96984cfc3ee4439f&nd=1&dlsi=5133fb386e2a4d9b.

4   Tobias Sturesson, "028. Hiltrud Werner: From Shock - to Shame - to Change," December 2020, in *Leading Transformational Change*, https://open.spotify.com/episode/4Ic1frmi9C9sV78WgCzAfI?si=5b739e722d-9243b7&nd=1&dlsi=b11bb6c07f0a4932.

5   Tobias Sturesson, "028. Margaret Heffernan: Mapping the Future and Avoiding Willful Blindness," December 2020, in *Leading Transformational Change*, https://open.spotify.com/episode/6I2t9khuziHr48J4aQjqWx?si=dOCoRvllQlWd9Ta_n7kgnQ&nd=1&dlsi=1d5a24af1534419c.

6   Stephen R. Covey, *The 7 Habits of Highly Effective People* (Rosetta Books, 1989), chap 3, Kindle.

7   Victor E. Frankl, *Man's Search for Meaning: The Classic Tribute to Hope from the Holocaust* (Beacon Press, June 1, 2006).

8   Tobias Sturesson, "081. Jay Barney: How Taking Ownership and Action Will Transform Your Culture with Jay Barney," November 2023, in *Leading Transformational Change,* https://open.spotify.com/episode/0QYTsTtkKolUaKN7pKkzF4?si=0dd20ec0bb7d4094.

9   Siobhan McHale, *The Insider's Guide to Culture Change: Creating a Workplace That Delivers, Grows, and Adapts* (HarperCollins Leadership, 2020), chap 6, Kindle.

Chapter 7

1   Sandra J. Sucher and Shalene Gupta, *The Power of Trust: How Companies Build It, Lose It, Regain It* (PublicAffairs, 2021), 25–27, Kindle.

2   Sucher and Gupta, *The Power of Trust*, 20, Kindle.

3   Tobias Sturesson, "016. Alison Taylor: Developing an Ethical Culture," June 2020, in *Leading Transformational Change*, https://open.spotify.com/episode/0YKGEiItylnn21IeipmT2x?si=7325f3a777104951.

4   Becky Kennedy, "The Single Most Important Parenting Strategy," April 2023, TED video, 14:04, https://www.ted.com/talks/becky_kennedy_the_single_most_important_parenting_strategy.

5   Daniel H. Pink, *The Power of Regret* (Penguin Publishing Group, 2022), chap 1, Kindle.

6   Tobias Sturesson, "053. Daniel Pink: Unlocking the Power of Regret," March 2022, in *Leading Transformational Change*, https://podcasts. apple.com/au/podcast/053-daniel-pink-unlocking-the-power-of-regret/ id1504162092?i=1000555069446.

7   Sucher and Gupta, *The Power of Trust*, 129, Kindle.

8   Tobias Sturesson, "064. Sandra J. Sucher: Trust: How Companies Build It, Lose It, Regain It," October 2022, in *Leading Transformational Change*, https://open.spotify.com/episode/1SGCbB8xZ1isKyp2ZOoLl2?si=adb523e eee424a69.

9   Sucher and Gupta, *The Power of Trust*, 133, Kindle.

Habit 2

1   Joshua L. Liebman, "Maturity is achieved when a person postpones immediate pleasures for long-term values," BrainyQuote, accessed February 2, 2024, https://www.brainyquote.com/quotes/joshua_l_liebman_132450.

Chapter 8

1   Frank Blake (former CEO of the Home Depot) in discussion with the author, May 21, 2018.

2   11Alive, "Arthur Blank Press Conference | Live Stream," Atlanta Falcons Training Camp, streamed live on August 1, 2023, YouTube video, 28:16, https://www.youtube.com/watch?v=yf6Djwx3LYQ.

3   Áine Cain, "Where's What Home Depot Looked Like When It First Opened in 1979," *Business Insider*, April 17, 2019, https://www.businessinsider.com/ home-depot-first-stores-photos-2019-4?r=US&IR=T#one-real-life-urban-legend-even-saw-a-manager-accepting-an-outlandish-return-17.

4   "Home Unimprovement: Was Nardelli's Tenure at Home Depot a Blueprint for Failure?" January 10, 2007, in *Knowledge at Wharton*, https://knowledge. wharton.upenn.edu/podcast/knowledge-at-wharton-podcast/home-unimprovement-was-nardellis-tenure-at-home-depot-a-blueprint-for-failure/.

5   Marc Hogan, "Big Box battle: Home Depot vs. Lowe's," NBC News, August 22, 2006, https://www.nbcnews.com/id/wbna14468345.

6   Frank Blake, "'A CEO Is Not Significant'—What Bernie Marcus Taught Me About Leadership," Crazy Good Turns, June 18, 2019, https://crazygoodturns.org/bernie-marcus-birthday#:~:text=You%20have%20a%20prominent%20job,we%20tend%20to%20forget%20that.

7   Tobias Sturesson, "068. Frank Blake: Culture Lessons from a Fortune 50 CEO," February 2023, in *Leading Transformational Change*, https://open.spotify.com/episode/4WuGVq9YAEwymheNMuZJbu?si=14b18c320a87424a.

8   "Highest Rated CEOs 2014 Employees' Choice," Glassdoor, 2014, https://www.glassdoor.com/Award/Highest-Rated-CEOs-2014-LST_KQ0,23.htm.

9   "From the Bottom Up," DistilINFO Retail, June 25, 2015, https://www.distilnfo.com/retail/2015/06/25/from-the-bottom-up/.

Chapter 9

1   "*A Hidden Life* (2019 film)," Wikipedia, accessed February 2, 2024, https://en.wikipedia.org/wiki/A_Hidden_Life_(2019_film).

2   Günter Bischof, "The Story of Austrian Catholic Resister Franz Jägerstätter," The National WWII Museum, April 11, 2019, https://www.nationalww2museum.org/war/articles/story-austrian-catholic-resister-franz-jagerstatter.

3   Tobias Sturesson, "038. Bianca Goodson & Mary Inman: Learnings from a Whistleblower," May 2021, in *Leading Transformational Change*, https://open.spotify.com/episode/0SAnlJpqEvjNLUjDXTUfIO?si=4953d9cf5aad42fe.

4   Tobias Sturesson, "056. Bo Rothstein: The Cost of Values & Building Trusted Institutions," May 2022, in *Leading Transformational Change*, https://open.spotify.com/episode/1hdSkQ6q0C5Dt8PENDjQTH?si=cfdb813c5b2b4c47.

5   Bill Saporito, "Boeing Made a Change to Its Corporate Culture Decades Ago. Now It's Paying the Price," *New York Times*, January 23, 2024, https://www.nytimes.com/2024/01/23/opinion/boeing-737max-alaska-airlines.html.

6   Tobias Sturesson, "039. Louise Bringselius: A Culture of Trust vs. Control," June 2021, in *Leading Transformational Change*, https://open.spotify.com/episode/28cfgbbfZDf8hk8MlIdiNP?si=82846b72165649b0.&nd=1&dlsi=69e857de5df04fdf.

7   Rushworth M. Kidder, *Moral Courage* (HarperCollins, 2006), 47.

8   Anna Dyląg, Waldemar Karwowski, Magdalena Jaworek, and Malgorzata Kozusznik, "Discrepancy between Individual and Organizational Values: Occupational Burnout and Work Engagement among White-Collar Workers," *International Journal of Industrial Ergonomics* 43, no. 3 (May 2013): 225–231, https://www.researchgate.net/publication/257036322_ Discrepancy_between_individual_and_organizational_values_ Occupational_burnout_and_work_engagement_among_white-collar_ workers.

9   Tobias Sturesson, "013. Carolyn Taylor: The Values-Driven Leader," April 2020, in *Leading Transformational Change*, https://open.spotify.com/episod e/0XwMQnMqMkZxeCzqOSkPYl?si=159436ee53de4717.&nd=1&dlsi=f5 b98ef5de59474d.

10   Tobias Sturesson, "063. Maria Hemberg: Leading with Values at Volvo Cars," October 2022, in *Leading Transformational Change*, https://open.spotify. com/episode/4WJDw9WDelDLV8zLohQdKr?si=06447d154a19434a&nd= 1&dlsi=27215f28950a4d9a.

11   Tobias Sturesson, "080. Design Your Company Culture to Connect with Values, Strategy, and Purpose with Melissa Daimler," October 2023, in *Leading Transformational Change*, https://open.spotify.com/episode/15tdL DaOwurbaIUMQluJ07.

Chapter 10

1   "Employers to Retain Half of Their Employees Longer if Bosses Showed More Appreciation; Glassdoor Survey," Glassdoor, November 13, 2013, https://www.glassdoor.com/employers/blog/employers-to-retain-half-of-their-employees-longer-if-bosses-showed-more-appreciation-glassdoor-survey/.

2   "Empowering Workplace Culture through Recognition," Gallup, accessed February 2, 2024, https://www.gallup.com/analytics/472658/workplace-recognition-research.aspx.

3   Tobias Sturesson, "035. Ed Schein & Peter Schein: Why Culture Change Isn't Working," April 2021, in *Leading Transformational Change*, https://open. spotify.com/episode/6B3x7oDNC899Oglvgx9Ygt?si=1b0a7c4655f14833.

4   Charles Duhigg, *The Power of Habit: Why We Do What We Do, and How to Change* (Random House, 2012), 100, Kindle.

5   Jon R. Katzenbach, James Thomas, and Gretchen Anderson, *The Critical Few* (Berrett-Koehler Publishers, 2019), 18, Kindle.

6   Tobias Sturesson, "021. Rob Chesnut: Intentional Integrity," September 2020, in *Leading Transformational Change*, https://open.spotify.com/episod e/4MMD1bxlmeitYuK2AmTHsP?si=3b480a8af9e04ded.

7   Richard M. Ryan and Edward L. Deci, "Self-Determination Theory and the Facilitation of Intrinsic Motivation, Social Development, and Well-Being,"*American Psychologist* 55, no. 1 (January 2000): 68–78, https://selfdeterminationtheory.org/SDT/documents/2000_RyanDeci_SDT.pdf.

Chapter 11

1   Per J. Andersson, "När Röda Korset förlorade hedern," OmVärlden, December 15, 2014, https://www.omvarlden.se/reportage/nar-roda-korset-forlorade-hedern.

2   "Röda Korset berättar: Förskingringen av Röda Korsets pengar 2009," Svenska Röda Korset. Förskiningen av Röda Korsets pengar 2009, accessed February 2, 2024, https://www.rodakorset.se/om-oss/ekonomi/forskingringen-av-roda-korsets-pengar-2009/.

3   Alexander Alonso, "Workplace Culture Matters," SHRM, *HR Magazine*, November 26, 2019, https://www.shrm.org/topics-tools/news/hr-magazine/workplace-culture-matters.

4   Donald Sull, Charles Sull, William Cipolli, and Caio Brighenti, "Why Every Leader Needs to Worry About Toxic Culture," MIT Sloan Management Review, March 16, 2022, https://sloanreview.mit.edu/article/why-every-leader-needs-to-worry-about-toxic-culture/.

5   Tobias Sturesson, "075. Charlie Sull: What It Takes to Build a Remarkable Culture - Learnings from the World's Largest Culture Study," August 2023, in *Leading Transformational Change*, https://podcasts.apple.com/fr/podcast/075-charlie-sull-what-it-takes-to-build-a/id1504162092?i=1000623997329.

6   Nicole Torres, "It's Better to Avoid a Toxic Employee than Hire a Superstar," *Harvard Business Review*, December 9, 2015, https://hbr.org/2015/12/its-better-to-avoid-a-toxic-employee-than-hire-a-superstar&sa=D&source=docs &ust=1699248268023270&usg=AOvVaw2ERmt-FWj9oC_jB6uPeqvw.

7   Toby Keel, "Armstrong Faces Woman He Smeared as 'Alcoholic Whore,'" Eurosport, November 18, 2013, https://www.eurosport.com/cycling/armstrong-faces-woman-he-smeared-as-alcoholic-whore_sto4011540/story.shtml.

8   BBC News, "Lance Armstrong: 'I'd probably cheat again,'" January 26, 2015, YouTube video, 5:31, https://www.youtube.com/watch?v=wzvZNQKowMU.

9   Deepa Purushothaman and Lisen Stromberg, "Leaders, Stop Rewarding Toxic Rock Stars," *Harvard Business Review*, April 20, 2022, https://hbr.org/2022/04/leaders-stop-rewarding-toxic-rock-stars.

10   Deepa Purushothaman, Rha Goddess, Billie Jean King, Dr. Sofia B. Pertuz, Therésè O'Higgins, Ashley Wells, Ellen Chamberlain, Lisen Stromberg, Lori Davis, Michele Madansy, and Noni Allwood, "PowHER Redefined: Women of Color Reimagining the World of Work," nFormation, Billie Jean King Leadership Initiative, accessed February 2, 2024, https://www.powherredefined.com/s/PowHER-Redefined-White-Paper.pdf.

11   Mickey Butts, "How Narcissistic Leaders Infect Their Organizations' Cultures," Berkeley Haas, October 3, 2020, https://newsroom.haas.berkeley.edu/research/how-narcissistic-leaders-infect-their-organizations-culture/.

12   Adam Grant, "Withholding feedback is choosing comfort over growth. Staying silent deprives people of the opportunity to learn," LinkedIn post, 2022, https://www.linkedin.com/posts/adammgrant_withholding-feedback-is-choosing-comfort-activity-6802225987963695104-c_oT/.

13   Kim Scott, *Radical Candor: How to Get What You Want by Saying What You Mean* (Pan Macmillan, 2017), chap 2, Kindle.

14   "Improve Talent Development with Our SBI Feedback Model," Center for Creative Leadership, November 24, 2022, https://www.ccl.org/articles/leading-effectively-articles/sbi-feedback-model-a-quick-win-to-improve-talent-conversations-development/.

Habit 3

1   Andy Stanley, "Leaders who refuse to listen will eventually be surrounded by people who have nothing significant to say," Twitter, accessed February 2, 2024, https://twitter.com/AndyStanley/status/103841035108630528.

Chapter 12

1   Kristina Lindh, "Visselblåsarna bakom Macchiarini-skandalen blev utfrysta," *Vi*, May 2017, https://www.vi.se/artikel/visselblasarna-bakom-macchiarini-skandalen-blev-utfrysta.

2   Karl-Henrik Grinnemo (surgeon) in discussion with the author, 2023.

3   Adam Ciralsky, "The Celebrity Surgeon Who Used Love, Money, and the Pope to Scam an NBC News Producer," *Vanity Fair*, January 5, 2016, https://www.vanityfair.com/news/2016/01/celebrity-surgeon-nbc-news-producer-scam.

4   "Let's Celebrate Whistleblowers," Transparency International, April 29, 2016, https://blog.transparency.org/2016/04/29/lets-celebrate-whistleblowers/index.html.

5   Tobias Sturesson, "037. Jim Detert: Choosing Courage," May 2021, in *Leading Transformational Change*, https://open.spotify.com/episode/3UIxm Uaurg1RlNEnpFaxhg?si=c483c9b0206b42ee.

6   Tobias Sturesson, "038. Bianca Goodson & Mary Inman: Learnings from a Whistleblower," May 2021, in *Leading Transformational Change*, https://open.spotify.com/episode/0SAnlJpqEvjNLUjDXTUfIO?si=8c26c09aa12e4 174.&nd=1&dlsi=b9394331433a4c83.

Chapter 13

1   Tobias Sturesson, "037. Jim Detert: Choosing Courage," May 2021, in *Leading Transformational Change*, https://open.spotify.com/episode/3UIxm Uaurg1RlNEnpFaxhg?si=c483c9b0206b42ee.

2   Mary C. Gentile, *Giving Voice to Values: How to Speak Your Mind When You Know What's Right* (Yale University Press, 2010), 202, Kindle.

3   Megan Reitz and John Higgins, *Speak Up* (FT Publishing International, 2019), 34, Kindle.

4   Tobias Sturesson, "057. Megan Reitz: A Culture of Speaking Up & Listening Up," May 2022, in *Leading Transformational Change*, https://open.spotify.com/episode/5shDOOsUt34vkMkzFjczqe?si=3041e8ba1c1147ec.

5   Reitz and Higgins, *Speak Up*, 57, Kindle.

6   Tobias Sturesson, "054. Kim Scott: Building a Culture of Compassionate Candor & Just Work," April 2022, in *Leading Transformational Change*, https://open.spotify.com/episode/5AL7m5xl0WgEB1UUKwNWam?si=b56 e19a9197f48b2.&nd=1&dlsi=0153a72f570a4fc0.

7   Kim Scott, "Asking for Feedback: How to Solicit Radical Candor," Medium, June 9, 2023, https://kimmalonescott.medium.com/asking-for-feedback-how-to-solicit-radical-candor-823dab2860c0.

Chapter 14

1   Larry Kim, "The Results of Google's Team-Effectiveness Research Will Make You Rethink How You Build Teams," Medium, December 26, 2017, https://medium.com/the-mission/the-results-of-googles-team-effectiveness-research-will-make-you-rethink-how-you-build-teams-902aa61b33.

2   Amy C. Edmondson, *The Fearless Organization: Creating Psychological Safety in the Workplace for Learning, Innovation, and Growth* (John Wiley & Sons, 2018), chap 1, Kindle.

3   Timothy R. Clark, *The 4 Stages of Psychological Safety: Defining the Path to Inclusion and Innovation* (Berrett-Koehler Publishers, 2020), chap preface, Kindle.

4   Whitney Smith, "Adam Kahane on Collaborating with the Enemy," Wild Culture, April 18, 2021, https://www.wildculture.com/article/adam-kahane-collaborating-enemy/1795.

5   Tobias Sturesson, "032. Adam Kahane: Bridge Differences and Facilitate Breakthrough," February 2021, in *Leading Transformational Change*, https://open.spotify.com/episode/4YipDzOKhaIDEoRUeUke3l?si=85a874 1be2044a16.

6   Fred Dust. *Making Conversation: Seven Essential Elements of Meaningful Communication* (HarperCollins, 2020), 14, Kindle.

7   "Stinky Fish," Hyper Island, accessed February 2, 2024, https://toolbox. hyperisland.com/stinky-fish-13d9ce8d-e64f-4085-8a06-8d212c627788.

Chapter 15

1   Tobias Sturesson, "020. Mary Gentile: Giving Voice to Values," August 2020, in *Leading Transformational Change*, https://open.spotify.com/episode/7vM yLR7ZuAC5i7yhKBCbpl?si=966cca35c5884e6c.

2   Gentile, *Giving Voice to Values*, 47, Kindle.

3   Mary C. Gentile, "Giving Voice to Values," accessed February 2, 2024, https://givingvoicetovaluesthebook.com/.

4   Jim Detert, *Choosing Courage* (Harvard Business Review Press, 2021), 87–172, Kindle.

5   Tobias Sturesson, "037. Jim Detert: Choosing Courage," May 2021, in *Leading Transformational Change*, https://open.spotify.com/episode/3UIxm Uaurg1RlNEnpFaxhg?si=c483c9b0206b42ee.

6   Tobias Sturesson, "020. Mary Gentile: Giving Voice to Values," August 2020, in *Leading Transformational Change*, https://open.spotify.com/episode/7vM yLR7ZuAC5i7yhKBCbpl?si=966cca35c5884e6c.

7   Gentile, *Giving Voice to Values*, Kindle.

8   Sturesson, "021. Rob Chesnut: Intentional Integrity."

Habit 4

1   Brené Brown, *Dare to Lead: Brave Work. Tough Conversations. Whole Hearts.* (Random House, 2018), 228, Kindle.

Chapter 16

1   Stephen Badger, "Mars Launches Independent Economics of Mutuality Foundation," Mars, September 9, 2020, https://www.mars.com/news-and-stories/articles/economics-mutuality-foundation.

2   Jay Jakub, "The Roots of the Economics of Mutuality," Oxford University Press, March 2021, https://academic.oup.com/book/39548/chapter/339404481.

3   Victoria Mars, "Defining the Role of Business in Five Principles: Victoria Mars, Mars Inc.," PwC, 2018, accessed February 2, 2024, https://www.pwc.com/gx/en/services/family-business/family-business-survey-2018/mars.html.

4   Bruno Roche and Jay Jakub, *Completing Capitalism: Heal Business to Heal the World* (Berrett-Koehler Publishers, 2017), 5, Kindle.

5   Hannah Radvan and Jeanne Roche, "Mars, Incorporated: Maua Programme." Mars Catalyst, May 2017, https://www.sbs.ox.ac.uk/sites/default/files/2018-06/mars_maua_-_mutuality_case_study_13.10.17.pdf.

6   Tobias Sturesson, "030. Jay Jakub: Putting Purpose at the Center of Your Business," January 2021, in *Leading Transformational Change*, https://open.spotify.com/episode/71c2sAX6Mv7dW2SnWWoyUy?si=15c6055c3d734601.&nd=1&dlsi=d6a25fbc4b554f1a.

7   "Reengineering Capitalism through Relationships," Economics of Mutuality, accessed February 2, 2024, https://eom.org/royal-canin.

8   Tobias Sturesson, "040. Colin Mayer: Putting Purpose into Practice," August 2021, in *Leading Transformational Change*, https://open.spotify.com/episode/1aTX5ZgAErlMBeBfHOFC54?si=54ee0d36676648b0&nd=1&dlsi=244c76d05c274471.

9   Dan Schawbel, "Mars CEO Grant Reid: Maintaining a Corporate Culture over 100 Years," *Forbes*, November 10, 2017, https://www.forbes.com/sites/danschawbel/2017/11/10/mars-ceo-grant-reid-maintaining-a-corporate-culture-over-100-years/?sh=674fea886f89.

10   Brett Ryder, "Mars Inc. Gets the Purpose v. Profit Balance Right," *Economist*, June 30, 2022, https://www.economist.com/business/2022/06/30/mars-inc-gets-the-purpose-v-profit-balance-right.

11   "Best Places to Work," Glassdoor, accessed February 2, 2024, https://www.glassdoor.com/Award/Best-Places-to-Work-2022-LST_KQ0,24.htm.

12   "Flint Water Crisis," National Center for Environmental Health, May 28, 2020, https://www.cdc.gov/nceh/casper/pdf-html/flint_water_crisis_pdf.html.

13   "Integrity," Wikipedia, accessed February 2, 2024, https://en.wikipedia.org/wiki/Integrity.

14   Luigi Guiso, Paola Sapienza, and Luigi Zingales, "The Value of Corporate Culture," *Journal of Financial Economics* 117, no. 1 (July 2015): 60–76, https://www.sciencedirect.com/science/article/abs/pii/S0304405X14001147.

Chapter 17

1   "Anne Margrethe Strømsheim," Trondheim.no, accessed February 2, 2024, https://www.trondheim.no/en/history/anne-margrethe-stromsheim.

2   Sue Monk Kidd, *The Secret Life of Bees* (Viking Penguin, 2002), 110, Kindle.

3   Tobias Sturesson, "027. Jennifer Chatman: The 4Cs of Healthy & Adaptive Culture," December 3, 2020, in *Leading Transformational Change*, https://open.spotify.com/episode/3iy5ZCskOX6ZZ3orETx3Oy?si=dd7f9ceb78664204.

4   "Marshall Ganz Quotes and Wisdom about Leadership, Hope, Organizing, and Narrative," The Commons, accessed February 2, 2024, https://commonslibrary.org/marshall-ganz-quotes-and-wisdom/.

5   Tobias Sturesson, "055. Mark Mortensen: Building Healthy Culture in a Hybrid World," April 2022, in *Leading Transformational Change*, https://open.spotify.com/episode/6TbueD6idlPoFEfFmw7xJU?si=9f0a613072b04e e3&nd=1&dlsi=2954c69f8b5c44b1.

6   Tobias Sturesson, "043. Guido Palazzo: Avoiding Ethical Tunnel Vision," October 2021, in *Leading Transformational Change*, https://open.spotify. com/episode/7CPUv6h5WYAEzN8J9YSYAO?si=e3e6215f1a384f7a&nd=1 &dlsi=629eab842cf34135.

7   Simon Carraud, "French Telco Orange Found Guilty over Workers' Suicides in Landmark Ruling," Reuters, December 20, 2019, https://www.reuters. com/article/us-france-justice-orange-sentences-idUSKBN1YO12D/.

8   Curt Nickisch and Jonathan Gottschall, "The Positives—and Perils— of Storytelling," February 8, 2022, in *HBR IdeaCast*, https://hbr.org/ podcast/2022/02/the-positives-and-perils-of-storytelling.

9   Justin Buzzard, "What's Your Story?" Christianity Today, June 17, 2013, https://www.christianitytoday.com/pastors/2013/june-online-only/whats-your-story.html.

10   Jay B. Barney, Manoel Amorim, and Carlos Júlio, *The Secret of Culture Change* (Berrett-Koehler Publishers, 2023), 39, Kindle.

11   Henry Mintzberg, "Musings on Management." *Harvard Business Review*. July–August 1996. https://hbr.org/1996/07/musings-on-management.

Chapter 18

1   Daniel M. Cable, *Alive at Work: The Neuroscience of Helping Your People Love What They Do* (Harvard Business Review Press, 2018), 119–120.

2   Cable, *Alive at Work*, 116.

3   Tobias Sturesson, "062. Dan Cable: Connecting People with Purpose," September 2022, in *Leading Transformational Change*, https://open.spotify. com/episode/5x9mXbFF9aV55uKwQxOoqK?si=2e2ec22040f94508&nd=1 &dlsi=f5a765b4ff1b48db.

4   Kyle Benson, "6 Hours a Week to a Better Relationship," The Gottman Institute, accessed February 2, 2024, https://www.gottman.com/blog/6-hours-a-week-to-a-better-relationship/.

5   John M. Gottman, *Eight Dates: Essential Conversations for a Lifetime of Love* (Workman Publishing Company, 2019), 188.

6   Edgar H. Schein and Peter A. Schein, *Organizational Culture and Leadership* (John Wiley & Sons, 1985), 11, Kindle.

7   Kevin M. Kniffin, Brian Wansink, Carol M. Devine, and Jeffery Sobal, "Eating Together at the Firehouse: How Workplace Commensality Relates to the Performance of Firefighters," *Human Performance* 28, no. 4 (2015): 281–306, https://www.tandfonline.com/doi/full/10.1080/08959285.2015.1 021049.

8   Deb Mashek, *Collabor(h)ate: How to Build Incredible Collaborative Relationships at Work (Even If You'd Rather Work Alone)* (Practical Inspiration Publishing, 2023), 56, Kindle.

9   Tobias Sturesson, "070. Deb Mashek: Why Collaboration Sucks and What to Do about It," March 2023, in *Leading Transformational Change*, https:// open.spotify.com/episode/52r7mudsHhFcDfAvEo55rT?si=d904d95eccde4f 7e&nd=1&dlsi=99b8b485911c4a91.

10   Carey Nieuwhof, "516. Michael McCain on Recruiting the Top Talent, the Problem with Short-Term Leadership Thinking," August 2022, in *The Carey Nieuwhof Leadership Podcast*, https://open.spotify.com/episode/2kcq8AN8 DYsF9bJZpUZ3ys?si=93904e4fa87c480f.&nd=1&dlsi=c3512999248b4587.

11   Andrew Hill, "C&A's Giny Boer: 'What We Want to Do Now Is Democratise Sustainable Fashion,'" September 4, 2022, https://www.ft.com/content/ a69405e1-acab-4d93-b816-a51730c5b417.

12   Priya Parker, *The Art of Gathering* (Penguin Books, 2018), 53, Kindle.

13   Steven G. Rogelberg, "Make the Most of Your One-on-One Meetings," *Harvard Business Review*, November–December 2022, https://hbr. org/2022/11/make-the-most-of-your-one-on-one-meetings.

14   Tobias Sturesson, "083. Why One-on-One Meetings Are Vital to Cultural Health and How to Make Them Better with Steven Rogelberg," December 14, 2023, in *Leading Transformational Change*, https://open.spotify.com/epi sode/3Cxqz0LHh9mRxzNRIcIyUE?si=774cea6bb82645b6&nd=1&dlsi=ff 8344ff959244fc.

Chapter 19

1   "American Customer Satisfaction Index Scores for Leading Quick Service Restaurant Chains in the United States in 2023, by Restaurant Brand," Statista, August 30, 2023, https://www.statista.com/statistics/194988/cus tomer-satisfaction-with-us-limited-service-restaurants-since-2006/.

2   Todd Starnes, "Chick-fil-A Gives Free Food to Motorists Stranded in Southern Snowstorm," Fox News, January 29, 2014, https://www.foxnews.com/opinion/chick-fil-a-gives-free-food-to-motorists-stranded-in-southern-snowstorm.

3   "How Employees Talk about Culture at Chick-fil-A," Culture 500, accessed February 2, 2024, https://sloanreview.mit.edu/culture500/company/c215/Chick_fil_A.

4   Bill Murphy Jr., "How People with High Emotional Intelligence Use the 'Chick-fil-A Rule' to Make Much Better Decisions" *Inc.*, August 27, 2022, https://www.inc.com/bill-murphy-jr/how-people-with-high-emotional-intelligence-use-the-chick-fil-a-rule-to-make-much-better-decisions.html.

5   Hayley Peterson, Alexandra York, and Nancy Luna, "What It Costs to Open 12 of the Biggest Fast-Food Chains in the US, including Chick-fil-A, McDonald's, and Taco Bell," *Business Insider*, March 21, 2023, https://www.businessinsider.com/mcdonalds-chick-fil-a-taco-bell-fast-food-franchise-costs-2019-5?r=US&IR=T#kfc-14-million-to-28-million-7.

6   "Best Places to Work," Glassdoor, accessed February 2, 2024, https://www.glassdoor.com/Award/Best-Places-to-Work-2022-LST_KQ0,24.htm.

7   Dee Ann Turner (vice president of corporate talent at Chick-fil-A) in discussion with the author.

8   Dee Ann Turner, *It's My Pleasure: The Impact of Extraordinary Talent and a Compelling Culture* (Elevate Publishing, 2015), part 1, Kindle.

9   Richard Bistrong, "A Journey from Corruption to Compliance," accessed February 2, 2024, https://www.richardbistrong.com/about.

10 Tobias Sturesson, "023. Richard Bistrong: Integrity on the Front-Lines," October 2020, in *Leading Transformational Change*, https://open.spotify.com/episode/7L97o5GG77ZcTVQNiq6bNA?si=081be4dbcb4c41d1&nd=1&dlsi=87691cd58694449e.

11 Schein and Schein, *The Corporate Culture Survival Guide*, 73, Kindle.

12 Schein and Schein, *The Corporate Culture Survival Guide*, 73, Kindle.

13 Tobias Sturesson, "033. Ron Carucci: Rehumanizing Organizations through Truth, Justice, and Purpose," March 2021, in *Leading Transformational Change*, https://open.spotify.com/episode/5tr15bbNVGIgPWpemWvTYF?si=30ed1dde7adc416e.&nd=1&dlsi=08633ce3e5784148.

14 "Re-Engineering Performance Management," Gallup, accessed February 2, 2024, https://www.gallup.com/workplace/238064/re-engineering-performance-management.aspx?thank-you-report-form=1.

15   Dori Meinert, "Is It Time to Put the Performance Review on a PIP?" SHRM, April 1, 2015, https://www.shrm.org/topics-tools/news/hr-magazine/time-to-put-performance-review-pip.

16   Tobias Sturesson, "069. Uri Gneezy: Avoiding Mixed Signals - How to Align Incentives With Values," February 2023, *Leading Transformational Change*, https://open.spotify.com/episode/43qcpvXP6Naq7dlRHM4Ww0?si=5540d fcf7d894f95.&nd=1&dlsi=66082d2242bd4027.

Conclusion

1   Ernest Hemingway, *The Sun Also Rises* (Scribner's, 1926), 136.

Acknowledgments

I never could have imagined how difficult, yet rewarding it would be to write this book.

I anticipated a yearlong endeavor. It stretched into seven. I thought I had the answers, only to discover I had much to learn. I believed I knew how to write but learned that I had yet to find my voice. I assumed I had moved beyond my past but realized I still had to fully process and embrace my story.

One thing is clear. This book owes its existence to many who provided insight, encouragement, mentoring, and generous support along the way.

It's with great joy and a deep sense of gratitude that I finally have the opportunity to extend my heartfelt thanks.

To the managers, executives, HR, and ethics and compliance professionals we've served: your successes, experiences, and struggles have taught me immensely. Thank you for your commitment to cultural health and for giving my team and I the honor of supporting your journey. You are our heroes!

To the many brilliant researchers, executives, and thought leaders who have been so remarkably generous with your time, knowledge, and support for the *Leading Transformational Change* podcast and this book: Frank Blake, Siobhan McHale, Jennifer Chatman, Stan Slap, Carolyn Taylor, Ann Tenbrunsel, Hiltrud Werner, Margaret Heffernan, Lenny Wong, Bob Langert, Daniel H. Pink, Colin Mayer, Giovanni Leoni, Rob Chesnut, Kalle Grinnemo, Jim Detert, Megan Reitz, Kim Scott, Mary Gentile, Mark Mortensen, Guido Palazzo, Dan Cable, Dee Ann Turner, Uri Gneezy, Maria Hemberg, Jay Barney, Sandra Sucher, Melissa Daimler, Mary Inman, Charlie Sull, Fred Dust, Adam Kahane, Aga Bajer, and Steven Rogelberg. My conversations with each of you have been invaluable, and I am immensely thankful for your contributions to the fields of management, culture, and ethics and for the opportunity to collaborate with you.

A special acknowledgment to the late Professor Emeritus Edgar Schein, who passed before this book's publication. Your insights into the nuances of culture and advocacy for humility and listening have guided me and countless others.

To Andreas Almlöf, our first external hire at Heart Management: thank you for all your wise input, encouragement, and support. Your commitment to cultural health and service to our clients has profoundly impacted me.

To Ron Carucci, Alison Taylor, Louise Bringselius, and Richard Bistrong: your generosity and encouragement were pivotal at the start of the *Leading Transformational Change* podcast and have sustained me throughout.

Celina Mina: thank you for helping me find my voice and always encouraging me to keep on writing.

Michaela Ahlberg and Anna Romberg, collaborating on a

global responsible leadership program was a great honor, a lot of fun, and a significant learning experience. Thank you for teaching me that friction is a good thing.

Jan Sturesson, Poul Dalgaard and Tim and Marsha Judy: you've been trusted mentors and advisors in different seasons of my life. I'm grateful for the opportunity to stand on your shoulders.

To Michael Snell and Kathy Sweeney, for taking the time to read and providing critical industry expertise at the right time.

To Chas Hoppe and Emily Gindlesparger: even though our collaboration didn't turn out the way we had hoped, you played a vital role in helping me structure the message and move the book forward.

Naren Aryal, Jenna Scafuri, and the awesome team at Amplify Publishing Group: you championed this project, offered an excellent path forward, and brought this book into the world. Thank you!

To André Noël Chaker, the best speaking coach one could ask for: you helped me simplify my message and clarify my audience.

To my best man and brother-in-arms, Kees Van Velzen: your unwavering support and wise counsel were indispensable every step of the way.

To kind and trusted friends and family who provided support, encouragement, laughter, and valued input along the way, including Daniel Sturesson, Johanna Sturesson, Matilda Johansson, Stefan Johansson, Toril Berg, Jan-Erik Berg, Liv Walla, Robert Walla, Elof Grahn, Desirée Grahn, Magnus Dahlberg, Georg Eidem, Mikael Nordvall, Emily Svensson, Gabriela Lomeu Campos, Simon Holmgren, Daniel Månsson, Nino Mireska, Andrew Mina, Rodrigo Correa, Debora Correa, Malachi Arunda, Jeffrey Miller, Theresa Grant, Morten Kroslid, Terentia Browne, Theresa Haynes, Felix Molonfalean, Kip Haynes, and many more.

To my parents, Margaretha and Sven Sturesson, for instilling in me a longing for righteousness and justice and for modeling the miracle of restoration.

To my parents-in-law (and love), Harald and Kari Haraldsen, for being wonderful examples of boundless love and generosity.

To my children, Eleonora, William, and Juliana: being your dad is my greatest honor and biggest joy. I am immensely proud of who you are. Thank you for allowing me to write this book. I hope it, in some small way, will help create a better world for you and your future families.

To the love of my life, my wife, Lena Sturesson: this book is as much your accomplishment as it is mine. You encouraged me to start this journey. You have sacrificed more than anyone will ever know to enable me to spend hundreds of hours researching and writing. You gave me courage when I wanted to give up. Believed in me when I didn't. Helped me process the pain of my past and realize that I was both known and loved. You model values-driven leadership every day.

Finally, to the rabbi and carpenter who washed people's feet, modeled what true leadership is all about, and paid the ultimate price for the sake of love and justice. I am forever grateful. If we could only learn to follow Your example.

> *"You know that the rulers in this world lord it over their people, and officials flaunt their authority over those under them. But among you it will be different. Whoever wants to be a leader among you must be your servant . . ."*
> —Matthew 20:25–26 (NLT)

About the Author

Having grown up in a religious cult and later confronted its toxic culture, **Tobias Sturesson** evolved into a prominent advocate for the vital importance of cultural health for organizational success and human flourishing. His advice is sought-after by leaders facing their most daunting culture challenges, whether navigating rapid growth or dealing with the fallout of a highly publicized scandal.

As the cofounder of Heart Management, a culture change agency, he has designed high-impact culture and leadership programs and trained thousands in values-driven leadership globally. His clients include many purpose-driven large corporations and organizations. Tobias hosts the top-ranked *Leading Transformational Change* podcast, featuring biweekly conversations with renowned researchers, executives, and experts on culture, management, and ethics.

A native of Sweden, Tobias finds inspiration from exploring the world with his family.